INFLATION AND THE MONETARIST CONTROVERSY

HARRY G. JOHNSON

Professor of Economics, The London School of Economics
and the University of Chicago
Visiting Professor, Institute for Advanced Studies
Vienna, September 1971

1972
NORTH-HOLLAND PUBLISHING COMPANY
AMSTERDAM – LONDON

© – NORTH-HOLLAND PUBLISHING COMPANY – 1972

All rights reserved. No part of this publication may be reproduced, stored in a retrieval system, or transmitted, in any form or by any means, electronic, mechanical, photocopying, recording or otherwise, without the prior permission of the copyright owner.

ISBN: 0 7204 3408 4

PRINTED IN THE NETHERLANDS

CONTENTS

G
229
J578

185957

Professor F. de Vries (1884–1958) became the first professor of economics at the Netherlands School of Economics (Rotterdam), which was founded in 1913. In 1945 he accepted an offer of the University of Amsterdam to teach economics in its Faculty of Law. On the occasion of his 70th birthday, May 2, 1954, his pupils created the Prof. F. de Vries Foundation to honour a most influential teacher and a scholar of outstanding theoretical and practical wisdom.

The aim of the foundation is regularly to invite prominent economists from abroad for a series of lectures on theoretical subjects, as a stimulus to theoretical work in economics in the Netherlands.

INTRODUCTION

Harry Gordon Johnson studied economics at the universities of Toronto, Cambridge and Harvard. After some minor teaching assignments he entered his brilliant academic career in 1950, as a Lecturer and Fellow of King's College, Cambridge. A Professor of Economic Theory at Manchester University from 1956–1959, he became Professor of Economics at the University of Chicago in 1959 and since 1966 combines this chair with a professorship at the London School of Economics and Political Science.

Thoroughly educated in the Keynesian tradition, yet, as a Canadian unlikely to be satisfied with the contemplation of a closed economy only, and later exposed to the full force of the Chicago school of monetarism, Professor Johnson had an excellent opportunity to establish himself as both an interpreter of, and an arbiter and bridge-builder between, diverging schools of economic thought. This he has accomplished in a masterly fashion, most particularly in the field on which I would dare to pass judgment, namely that of monetary theory and monetary policy. His *Essays in Monetary Economics* (1967) bear witness to his vast knowledge of the literature, his sound judgment and the lucidity of his exposition.

The Professor F. de Vries Foundation was very happy to find Professor Johnson willing to lecture at the University of Amsterdam on *Inflation and the*

Monetarist Controversy, because it considered this subject of particular relevance to a country which, notwithstanding so many excellent policy intentions, has of late been suffering increasingly from inflationary developments. I am confident that the present volume, containing the lectures given, will be found to clarify the issues for both theorists and policy makers.

M.W. Holtrop

PREFACE

As the lectures contained in this book themselves record, I was both honoured and challenged by the invitation to give the 1971 F. de Vries lectures in Amsterdam. I should like here to record my gratitude to the F. de Vries Foundation and the University of Amsterdam for the unobtrusively excellent arrangements they made for the lectures themselves, and for their hospitality. I am particularly grateful to Marius W. Holtrop for a memorable dinner party distinguished by the seriousness and high quality of the discussion of economic and university problems with my Dutch professional colleagues.

I would also like to express my gratitude to my friend and sometime colleague Mel Krauss, and his wife Irène, for their patient hospitality during a hectic weekend of lecture-polishing, and especially Irène for her kindness in typing the lectures from my nearly-illegible manuscript.

Harry G. Johnson

20th October 1971

CHAPTER I

THE PROBLEM OF INFLATION AND THE EVOLUTION OF MONETARY THEORY

May I begin by saying that I am greatly honoured to have been invited to deliver the de Vries Lectures this year. Professor de Vries was a distinguished member of a distinguished intellectual community, and the series of lectures established in his memory have performed the important function of making available, not only in the Netherlands but to the whole of the English-reading economics profession, the thoughts on and analyses of current economic problems of the western world's most eminent economists. This occasion happens to be my first actual visit to your country: no economist, however, could fail to be aware of the strong tradition of good economic scholarship here, or to have been influenced in his own thinking and writing by the works and professional presence of the leaders of the present genera-

1

tion of Dutch economists, resident and non-resident in the Netherlands — such as Jan Tinbergen, Marius Holtrop, Hans Theil, Hendrik Houthakker, Tjalling Koopmans, and Jacques Polak, to name only those who have had a direct and memorable influence on my own professional development.

It is, however, a rather daunting assignment to undertake to address a Netherlands audience of professional colleagues on the general question of the capacity of monetary policy to cope with inflation, since the economists of this country — as represented particularly by the monetary theorizing of J. G. Koopmans, J. Zijlstra, and M.W. Holtrop and the model of monetary analysis developed by the Netherlands Bank under the inspiration and leadership of the last-named [1] — have maintained a serious, scholarly and practical interest in the monetary approach to the theory and practice of economic stabilization throughout a long period during which the predominant Anglo-Saxon tradition in economics — as a result of what I would judge a basic misinterpretation of the contributions of John Maynard Keynes [2] — has denigrated and dismissed the long-established insights of the monetary approach into the relation between monetary management and inflation in favour of an essentially *ad hoc* approach to the problem in terms of income—expenditure-cum-institutional analysis. The wheel has now come full circle, at least for the more open-minded and undoctrinaire members of the profession, and the intellectual integrity and scientific conservatism of the

Dutch monetary tradition is gaining increasing outside professional respect as colleagues in other countries realise that what appear to them as bold new monetarist theories are essentially nearly identical with the commonplace precepts of Dutch monetary theory. As the late Sir Dennis Robertson used to teach us in Cambridge when I was a student – I now confess, a rather uncomprehending one – "highbrow opinion is like a hunted hare; if you stand still long enough, it will come back to the place it started from".[3] Highbrow Anglo-Saxon monetary theory has just recently come back to the starting-point at which Dutch monetary theory has stayed – the Wicksellian concern with monetary equilibrium and the conditions for monetary neutrality, which reached its full intellectual flower in the early 1930's only to be swept into intellectual limbo by the Keynesian revolution.

As a typical representative of Robertson's highbrows, who has made the circuit from the traditional quantity theory of Harold Innis's University of Toronto through the sophisticated Keynesian economics of the Cambridge University of Joan Robinson and Richard Kahn (and later of Nicholas Kaldor) and the much less sophisticated Keynesian economics of Alvin Hansen's Harvard, to my current abodes in Milton Friedman's University of Chicago and Lionel Robbins's London School of Economics, I am profoundly aware that much of what I have to say about money and inflation will be only too well known to this audience. Nevertheless, both confirmation and rejection of hypotheses are deemed to be useful scientific activities; and it may be — or at least so I hope — that a new view of known problems will be provocative of new thought even though it turns out on reflection that most of the essential message is already well understood.

The problem of inflation, with which these lectures are concerned, has been a chronic problem of the 'western' or 'mixed free enterprise' economies throughout the postwar II period. This fact has been contrary to the almost universal late-wartime expectation, grounded in Keynesian theory and especially in the American Keynesian tradition established by Alvin Hansen, that the end of the war would be followed by a disastrous depression of 1930's dimensions unless drastic Keynesian expansionary policies were adopted. That expectation, it is evident in the blinding light of hindsight, overlooked the historical fact that, for reasons easily explainable in terms · of traditional monetary theory, major wars have inevitably been followed by severe inflations, for a varying but non-negligible period. It is also evident that the measures adopted for Keynesian reasons to cushion the expected deflation, especially large-scale deficit financing of war efforts at low interest rates supported by money creation and enforced in real terms by price and wage controls and physical rationing, made the immediate postwar wave of inflation more severe than it needed to have been. That particular wave of inflation was aggravated, for the European economies, by

4

the sequential coupling of the currency devaluations of 1949 — which appear, again in the light of hindsight, to have been excessive and to have contributed to the serious problem of international monetary disequilibrium that has plagued the capitalist world since the late 1950's — with the inflationary impact on primary product prices of the war in Korea. It is important for the maintenance of historical perspective to note that the inflation that has been concerning public opinion and policy makers in most countries in the past few years is attributable at least in important part to the same combination of factors — on the one hand, a major war measured in economic terms, financed by deficits and money creation rather than by taxes, and on the other hand currency devaluation or reluctance to appreciate under-valued currencies.

The fact that the chronic problem of the postwar western world has been inflation rather than mass unemployment is associated with the fact that on the average the countries comprising that world have maintained rates of economic activity and employment unprecedentedly high by interwar standards. Some would, and still do, attribute this eminently desirable accomplishment, and the economic growth that has gone with it, to the intellectual success of the Keynesian revolution in teaching governments the techniques of demand management, and the practical success of governments in applying those techniques. This explanation is highly implausible. On the one

5

hand, the Keynesian revolution in economic theory and policy making has had relatively little impact outside the two countries of its origin and major intellectual development — the United Kingdom and the United States — and it was less than a decade ago that the advent of the 'new economics', personified by Walter Heller's chairmanship of the Council of Economic Advisers, was hailed in the latter country, while even in the United States the governmental machinery is ill-adapted to the execution of Keynesian-style economics policies, to the extent that the timing of fiscal policy changes has generally been pro-cyclical rather than anti-cyclical. On the other hand, there are good reasons, rooted both in the 'real' analysis of the economic historians[4] and in monetary theory, as to why capitalist economies should be expected in normal circumstances both to maintain a high level of employment and to enjoy some non-negligible rate of economic growth. Put very briefly, 'real' analysis calls attention to the opportunities for the profitable investment of savings that the world of reality constantly throws up, while monetary analysis assumes as a matter of empirical fact that the economic system tends towards a rational full-employment allocation of resources so long as the management of money is well-behaved, and can only be thrown off-course by severe monetary mismanagement.

This latter assumption is, of course, in a sense the crux of the issue prevailing between Keynesians and monetarists: the Keynesian position is that the real economy is highly unstable and that monetary management has both little relevance to it and little control over it; the monetarist position on the contrary is that the real economy is inherently fairly stable, but can be destabilized by monetary developments, which therefore need to be controlled as far as possible by intelligent monetary policy. The monetarist position — in this very general sense, which leaves open all the important scientific questions about how monetary impulses affect the economy and how money should be managed — seems to me the only alternative consistent with the facts (as distinct from the myths) of historical experience. And though I do not wish at this particular point to go into the empirical evidence in detail, I should remark that I have arrived at this judgment, not by dogmatic conviction, but out of growing dissatisfaction with the explanatory power of the theories and the empirical results of the policies of Keynesian economics in which I was instructed during my youth at the two major centres of the revolution.

I should also remark, in passing, that I find not merely implausible but completely incredible two other variants of a Keynesian explanation of the success of the western capitalist world in maintaining high employment since the second world war, both of which rest on the Keynesian assumption that capitalism cannot prosper without a large and sustained exogenous — and preferably both irrational and immoral — demand for goods and services. One, which has appealed greatly in recent years to so-called intellectuals trained in the emotional and religious self-indulgences of vulgar Marxism, is the idea that the survival of capitalism depends on the wastage of vast amounts of resources in unjust imperialistic adventures in military aggression. This explanation deliberately disregards, or, more likely, is simply naively ignorant of, the economic implications of the considerable swings in levels of military expenditure that have occurred over the postwar period, in terms of their theory of capitalism. The other, which has recently been put into circulation by my former colleague Nicholas Kaldor in three prestigious articles in *The Times*[5], is the pseudo-monetary hypothesis that capitalism has been kept going in the postwar period by the willingness of the United States to inject an exogenous expansionary item of demand into the world economy by running a persistent and growing balance-of-payments deficit. Neither Kaldor's assertion that the United States has suffered sustained heavy unemployment as a result of this benevolent irrationality of its macro-economic policy, nor his assumption that a net demand injection of the order of $3 billion on average — a small fraction of a tenth of one per cent of total world output — has sufficed to make capitalism a success in the postwar period, can make any empirical sense to economists schooled in the scientific view that an idea is to be tested by its empirical relevance rather than by its intellectual brilliance.

Keynesian theory, then, offers no satisfactory explanation of why the quarter century since the second world war has been characterized by reasonably full employment in the capitalist countries, and therefore of why its chronic problem has been inflation rather than Keynesian mass unemployment. At most, Keynesian theory can offer an explanation, which incidentally is not Keynesian, but merely a Keynesian description of phenomena well understood by pre-Keynesian monetary theorists, of why high employment tends to generate price inflation. And even this description is marred, as I shall argue later, by the tendency of Keynesian theorists, following their master, to reason in terms of a closed economy and to ignore the linkings between price developments in the various countries of the world economic system created by the system of fixed exchange rates on the one hand and the maintenance of relatively liberal international trade and payments arrangements on the other. As a consequence, the problem of inflation has tended to appear in the literature as a series or collection of individual national problems, essentially sociological in origin, rather than as an international monetary problem.

In sum, neither the adoption of Keynesian stabilization policies by governments, nor the application of the simple Keynesian view that if capitalism is successful this must be attributable to some "uncapitalistic" exogenous demand factor, seems capable of explaining the sustained stability and prosperity of the world economy since the second world war. The broad facts fit much better with the traditional assumptions that the system possesses a great deal of inherent stability and that — though this anticipates subsequent argument — monetary factors play a determining role in the long-run development of prices and interest rates. The intellectual and popular success of the Keynesian revolution in economic theory has, however, nevertheless brought about a fundamental change in the atmosphere or climate of public opinion in the postwar period as compared with the prewar, a change vital for economic policy-making and specifically for the problem of inflation. This change consists simply in the general acceptance of the proposition that government has both the power and the responsibility to maintain a politically satisfactory level of employment. Moreover, by a not entirely logical connection of ideas based on the identification of new investment as the source of productivity increase, government has also come to be charged with the responsibility for maintaining a satisfactory rate of economic growth, while one natural consequence of the extension of governments' economic responsibilities has been that the maintenance of a satisfactory balance of payments has become a policy objective or at least a constraint on the pursuit of other policy objectives that must be satisfied. Thus, the standard list of policy objectives reeled off whenever appropriate by government and central bank spokesmen, official commissions, and independent policy commentators has come, even in the Netherlands, to consist of four items: high employment, economic growth, price stability, and a reasonable balance of payments. (Tastes vary internationally regarding the inclusion of a fifth objective, described in Canada as 'an equitable distribution of income'.)

The acceptance of 'full' or 'high' employment as an objective of government policy has been a fundamental change, with widespread implications of varying degrees of subtlety. One obvious implication, which was in fact recognized by a number of earlier Keynesian writers on economic policy, though against the background of the 1930's experience of mass unemployment they either played down the point and hoped for the best or were dismissed as inhumane and immoral dogmatists and preachers of doom, is that a serious government effort to maintain continuous full employment implies loss of policy control of the wage and prices levels, since the monetary authority will have to validate any wage and price increases determined by competitive pressures or — the more usual bogey — administrative price-fixing by oligopolistic firms and collective wage-bargaining involving oligopolistic unions.

This basic point, which has been elegantly formulated in particular by M.W. Reder [6] and J.R. Hicks [7], has persisted throughout subsequent discussions of the inflation problem in two specific forms. One has been the pragmatic recognition that the commitment both inclines the political policy-making process to take calculated risks on the inflationary consequences of demand-expansive policies, and obliges it to accept inflation once it has occurred rather than attempt to fight wages and prices back down towards their starting point. The other is a strong propensity, even among professional economists who should know better, to blame inflationary developments on the immoral self-seeking activities of monopolistic industries and unions. The elementary economic theory of value teaches that monopolies, either firms or unions, will seek to set a relative price for their product that maximizes profits in real terms, while monetary theory suggests that the money price so determined will be adjusted by rational maximizers in conformity with general changes in the price level, so as to maintain the maximizing real price relativity. (One has, however, to recognize a potentially important qualification here: If established businesses and union managements are slow to make adjustments to the fact of inflation, they may be challenged by more junior people in their organizations with the result that the organization comes to regard a higher relative real price for the product as the optimal profit-maximizing strategy; and, particularly in the case of 'union militancy', this may lead to efforts by rival organizations to restore traditional real price relativities through inflationary adjustments of money prices.) With this view of inflation as being due to the selfishness of monopolistic organizations, ungrateful for the politically-conferred benefits of full employment, naturally goes the pro-

12

pensity to prescribe an incomes policy of some kind as a panacea for inflation. And with that prescription comes the typical and insoluble dilemma of incomes policy: that its aim is to substitute for a politically-imposed constraint on the use of monetary policy against inflation, but that its implementation becomes embogged in the effort to correct real distortions in the operation of the competitive system, or even more hopelessly in the effort to distort the workings of competition in order to secure a more ethically satisfactory distribution of income.

A more subtle implication and one that is not recognized by the traditional Benthamite—Fabian approach to the nature and functions of government characteristic of economic policy theory and the theory of welfare economics, though it has increasingly been made the subject of the recently-evolving economic theory of government, and is recognized rather uneasily and uncomfortably by economists concerned with economic policy formation, is associated with the fact that, whatever the rhetoric of the public good involved, the prime problem of politicians is not to serve the public good but to get elected to office and remain in power. The knowledge both that the public holds them accountable for its experiences of unemployment and of inflation, and that they do have their hands on levers that influence these experiences, naturally suggests the use of these levers to maintain and strengthen political support among the electorate rather than to serve a larger-range concept of the pu-

13

blic good if the public finds what is good for it hard to live with. Specifically, politicians elected on the basis of promises of anti-inflationary policies who attempt to carry them out are under strong social-psychological pressures to abandon them in the face of their growing unpopularity and the approach of the next elections; and politicians facing an election they fear they may lose are under similarly strong pressures to inflate the economy to gain votes, in the expectation that if they win they will have time to clear up the mess they have created sufficiently soon for the public to forget their deceitfulness before the next elections, and that if they lose their opponents will come into office with a cripplingly embarrassing mess to clean up, any failures or unpleasantness involved in the effort constituting ammunition for the next election. This process has been evident in the United Kingdom and the United States in recent years; it is so well known in Europe as to have been christened 'the political cycle' (i.e. business or trade cycle).

A third, and still more subtle, implication, is one that is virtually universally disregarded in economic theorizing and model-building. It is associated with the fact that the effective economic decision-taking sector of the public is fairly fully aware of the political nature of and constraints on economic policy decisions, and uses this knowledge in its own decision-taking. Contrary to the standard assumptions of economic theory, the economic public does not simply respond mechanically, according to econometricallydetermined behaviour relationships, to signals reaching it through the blind and impersonal operations of price and quantity determination in competitive markets. Instead, the relevant economic public engages in two kinds of political transactions with its governmental policy-makers, both of a game-theoretic rather than atomistic-competition type. First, one of its major concerns is to guess how determined the government is about implementing its announced economic policies, and particularly how soon the government will be forced by the pressures of political unpopularity to reverse its policies before they have become clearly effective in securing their objectives. This has been a favourite subject of discussion in informed economic circles in both the United Kingdom and the United States in the past two years – with the British Government being able to hold out longer than the American because it had a longer run up to the next election, but with both sacrificing their policies to political pressures well before success was more than an optimistic possibility. Second, the relevant economic public, aware of the sensitivity of government to political pressures, has an incentive to generate such pressures in its own favour so far as it can, through both private representations and public pronouncements, the latter often of a contra-factual or contra-analytical nature.

The consequence of these implications of the commitment to 'full employment' as a policy objective is that academic analyses of the causes of inflation and of the relative merits of economic policies for dealing with it are to an important extent unreal. They are about knowledge and its limits, rather than about the uses to which society chooses to put its existing limited knowledge. Further, presumably scientific debates about economic policy are frequently poisoned — sometimes quite deliberately and intentionally — by the engagement of the economists concerned in the political process itself. The proclamation of politically unpalatable truth becomes an invitation to pseudo-scientific character assassination, while the invention of so-called 'boldly unorthodox' theories that seek to repeal the laws of economics because they stand in the way of the politicians' desire to maximize their political utility function without reference to the economic budget constraint becomes an avenue of professional advancement. Still, this is a fact of life with which scientifically-minded economists have to learn to live, in the hope that sometimes, or in the long run, truth will somehow prevail.

The fact that inflation has been a chronic problem of the western capitalist world for a quarter of a century implies that the processes of political decision-making have been in fact prepared to tolerate it as an element in a politically optimal system of economic management. There has been, in other words, a 're-vealed preference' for inflation. In view of the ostensible and often highly vocal political resistance to inflation and insistence on governmental responsibility for stopping or at least minimizing inflation, this is a

16

rather paradoxical situation. Economic theory suggests two alternative possible lines of explanation.

The first rests on a presumed irrationality of governmental decision-taking. There are three conceivable variants of this explanation.

The first, which I would regard as definitely untenable, is that government is simply ignorant of the causal factors in inflation and unaware of the inflationary consequences of its own policy choices.[8] This hypothesis is completely implausible, given both the sophistication of contemporary economic understanding and the fact that even politicians are capable of learning from their own and others' experience; and dismissal of it out of hand is not inconsistent with the observation that, for their own purposes, politicians frequently deny or attempt to deny that a particular policy action will have the inflationary consequences that such a policy action has always had in the past.

The second variant is that, in technical terms, the political preference function violates the standard axioms of consistency and transitivity, so that political preferences as revealed in actual decisional behaviour are inconsistent. This explanation is plausible as an observation based on governmental behaviour over relatively short periods of years, and can be supported by reference on the one hand to the responsiveness of politicians to political pressures emanating from the electorate, together with the fact that the public tends to complain most vociferously about whatever is currently annoying it most about its eco-

17

nomic situation, and on the other to the internal de-centralization of government policy-making, according to which two institutions with different traditions are assigned separately primary responsibility for what may be termed the 'real' and the 'monetary' aspects of policy, the Treasury being primarily responsible for employment and growth and the central bank for price stability and the balance of payments, with the results both that their policies may conflict and that now one and now the other achieves command in overall policy-making. The problem at hand, however, is not one of random inconsistency or alternation in the pursuit of policy objectives, but of a long-run systematic bias in the policy-making process towards an inflationary outcome.

This brings us to the third variant of this line of explanation, which is that the political decision-taking process is rational in its own terms, but systematically biased towards under-estimating the social value of price stability and the social costs of inflation. This explanation also can claim considerable plausibility on various grounds. One, already mentioned, is the necessary preoccupation of politicians elected for short terms of office with short-run achievements to the neglect of the longer-run consequences of their policies. If government were conducted in the same way as the management of the large industrial, commercial, and financial corporations, it would probably do much more, and much more intensive, long-range planning.[9] Another comes from the economic theory of democracy[10], which stresses the cost-benefit aspects of acquiring the information required for intelligent voting behaviour as explaining the dominance of producer over consumer interests in political decision-taking. In the context of the explanation of persistent inflation, the argument would be that the losses from inflation come on the side of consumption, and that two important classes of potential losers lack political organization as producer groups to defend their interests as consumers. These are, on the one hand, the retired and other socially-dependent groups who are out of the active labour force and do not currently produce the incomes on which they live, and on the other hand the numerically important group of the currently occupied who produce, not goods and services for the private market, but services for the governmental, educational, health-care, and other institutions of society and are subject both to the problems of confronting a monopoly purchaser and to ethico-sociological constraints on their capacity to pursue unashamedly their economic self-interests. This explanation, also, lacks plausibility in the longer run, for two economic reasons. First, a reason now familiar from the 'permanent-income' and 'life-savings' theories of consumption and the more general theory of human capital, rational active producers should appreciate that they will eventually themselves retire, and in the meantime may fall victim to life's various accidents, and so in their political behaviour have regard for the economic position of the ailing and the

19

retired — as in fact the political process does, through periodic revision of the monetary values of social security and retirement benefits. Second, one would expect that in the longer run the supply of employees to what may be loosely called the public sector would respond to the real income prospects there as compared with those in the private sector — including possible victimization by inflation; and in fact public sector salaries are also adjusted periodically to the fact of inflation.

The 'irrationality of government' explanations of inflation therefore, plausible as they may appear, do not hold up very convincingly as explanations of a long-sustained period of what may be termed 'creeping' or 'strolling' or 'briskly walking' rather than 'galloping' inflation. The alternative line of explanation assumes that, on a long-run average, government is both rational and informed about the alternatives confronting it, and broadly representative of the preferences of the public as a whole; and it attributes the revealed preference for inflation to the hypothesis that inflation of the kind under discussion has relatively little social cost and hence is not too irksome to tolerate as the price of achieving other economic objectives.

In contemplating this hypothesis, an economist has to be (or at least ought to be, since so few are) acutely aware of social and intellectual pressures to prejudge the issue in terms of emotional, political and social commitments. The pressures come from both sides.

On the one hand, the origins of Keynesian economics in interwar and still largely Victorian England predispose Keynesian economists — particularly those sequestered in the medieval environments of Oxford and Cambridge — to the belief that economic nirvana consists in everyone being fully employed in his allotted station in life, which implies that no price in terms of other economic disturbances is too high to pay for full employment. This is an attitude only too happily shared by the organized labour movement and by those who identify socialism with espousal of the conservative self-interests of 'the workers'. But economic rationality requires recognition that society has other interests with which those of full employment for workers may conflict, including some of the interests of the workers themselves, and that the social and economic costs of unemployment are a function of the other social policies that society chooses to adopt. 'Love on the Dole' meant misery and degradation in the 1930's in the North of England; in the 1960's it came to mean the liberty and economic irresponsibility of hippiedom in California.

On the other hand, the voices that speak against inflation and in favour of price stability as a policy objective are not to be trusted either. Concern about preservation of the purchasing power of money is characteristically the special responsibility of the financial community, headed by the central bank as that community's special representative in the governmental machinery. As such, it expresses the self-

21

interest of a vested interest group with no more claim to respect for its economic understanding than any other interest group. Much of the respect that its claims nevertheless command derives from the historically irrelevant circumstances of medieval history, when debasement of the currency by the monarch was a desperate last-resort method of taxing honest merchants and other commoners by deliberate fraud. There was, therefore, a need for a moral pressure group to keep the monarch honest (and frequently conveniently penurious) in defense of the hard-earned wealth of honest citizens. That logic does not apply to the modern world of democratically-selected governments, in which (except in the case of major wars, where outright confiscation of wealth and income is the only alternative to inflationary taxation) the main consequences of inflation are redistributions from one group of citizens to another — insofar as inflation can constitute a method of redistributory taxation, which theory suggests is doubtful in the longer run.

In recent times, however, partly as a result of the subordination of central bank policies to the fiscal needs of Treasuries, a major source of political complaint about inflation has come to be the consumer. Here the alert economist should observe and contemplate the economic implications of the contemporary institution of marriage, and particularly of the customary division of economic responsibilities between the husband as the earner of income and the wife as the household-utility-maximizing major spend-

22

er of it — an application of Adam Smith's principle of specialization and division of labour that only the advertising men and their economists have tried to accommodate to. This division of responsibility in the earning and spending of income, and particularly the time-lag in the adjustment of the husband's nominal budgetary allocations to his wife to the fact of inflation, besides making inflation a powerful enemy of the Women's Liberation Movement and guarantor of male supremacy, makes inflation a serious political issue for women, and to some extent for the more hen-pecked of their husbands, even though when the family balance-sheet is consolidated inflation may have a zero or positive effect on total family welfare. As politicians are well aware, men vote for jobs and women vote for lower prices.

If one can dodge these political opinion-traps, the scientific question for consideration is, what are the main elements in the economic costs of inflation. As already suggested, much of the argument about the evils of inflation concerns effects of inflation which may or may not be considered to be social costs, but which actually do not involve economic costs in the sense of waste of resources and sacrifice of potential consumption or investment — that is, redistributions of income from creditors to debtors, or from old age pensioners, social security recipients, and public sector employees to private sector employees and entrepreneurs, or from wives to husbands. With respect to the social costs — which incidentally are sometimes, at least as regards the first two, regarded as socially desirable rather than undesirable — economic theory suggests, first, that if they are considered serious they could be compensated by appropriate institutional changes, rather than requiring the battling of inflation by economic policy, and secondly that the institutional mechanisms of a society based on freedom of choice and competition will, if the system of contract is reasonably flexible and inflation not too erratic, act to bring about the elimination of major inflationary injustices. If one is to find genuine economic costs of inflation, therefore, one must look for costs that cannot or will not be eliminated by the processes of competitive contract adjustment.

One obvious problem arising from inflation, which has much exercised economists and economic policy in the contemporary era, has been its adverse balance-of-payments implications. This problem, however, has to be properly understood as a problem itself created by government policy, and moreover as one that has come to cut in the opposite direction to that formerly assumed, as the western world has become an inflationary environment. The standard argument against inflation based on external economic considerations is that inflation will render a country's export and import-competing goods internationally uncompetitive, and so face it with a balance-of-payments problem. But that problem is created not by inflation *per se* but by the government's tolerating domestic inflation while trying to adhere to a fixed exchange value of its

24

currency, which policy dishonestly pretends that the purchasing power of the currency is stable when in reality it is being eroded by the governmentally-tolerated inflation. And the economic losses associated with inflation are those imposed by government itself in its efforts to avoid admitting the inconsistency between its inflationary domestic policies and its fixed exchange rate, either by deflating its domestic economy severely occasionally in order to try to restore its international price competitiveness, or by imposing distorting restrictions on the international trade and payments of its citizens, thereby sacrificing the advantages of international specialization and division of labour, rather than by following the theoretically proper policy of devaluing its currency or allowing it to depreciate in order to reconcile internal inflation with external economic viability within a liberal trade and payments system. Moreover, for many countries in the contemporary inflationary world, external balance with a fixed exchange rate requires more or less deliberate inflation, to avoid the necessity of transferring real resources to more inflationary countries at the expense of the living standards and growth prospects of the domestic public. In the context of world inflation, domestic arguments against inflation, when not firmly allied with insistence on upwards exchange rate flexibility, are pleas for trying to hold back an inflation ultimately inevitable so long as the exchange rate remains fixed while other countries are inflating, by means of low-yield or negative-yield loans

25

of real domestic resources to foreigners.

Turning to domestically-oriented arguments against inflation, recent theorizing has turned up only two significant such arguments. The first, which rests on the assumption that inflation comes to be fairly rapidly anticipated, and so translated into the determination of money prices, wages and interest rates, which therefore preserve their real equilibrium values and relativities, stresses the costs and welfare losses arising from the inability of the public to recontract the holding terms on the one asset whose supply is monopolized by the government, namely money, along with money-substitute assets such as government debt and various kinds of savings media, the terms on which are controlled at least partially by the government. This cost, it can be shown by relatively simple empirical calculations, is likely to be trivial for mild inflations occurring in a financially advanced economy. The second economic argument against inflation, on the other hand, stresses the costs of acquiring information and taking decisions in the face of uncertainty about what the rate of inflation in fact will be. It should be noted that this aspect of the cost of inflation is not a cost of inflation as such, but a cost of variations in the trend of the general level of prices; and that consequently the costs of stopping inflation on this account may be greater than the costs of letting it continue at its current rate. Further, given the political constraints already mentioned on the capacity of government to adopt and to adhere to for long a sharp change of direction in economic policy, combined with the ability of the more important economic decision-takers to forecast trends and changes in government policy with some degree of reliability, the costs involved may be relatively small in advanced countries, though they may well be high indeed in less-developed countries with unstable governments.

These brief remarks reflect what I hope is a consensus of common-sense economics on the question of the costs of inflation of the kind experienced during the past twenty-five years. It may be useful, however, in concluding this lecture, to survey briefly what more formal monetary theory has had to say about the welfare aspects of inflation. As already mentioned, formal monetary theory up into the 1930's when the Keynesian revolution struck, was dominated by the Wicksellian concepts of monetary equilibrium and of 'neutral' money. The essential concern of that tradition was with the conditions under which money would remain merely a 'veil', in the neoclassical phrase, over the workings of the underlying barter economy, conditions which Wicksell summarized in the principles of equality of the real and money rates of interest, equality of (ex ante) savings and investment, and stability of the price level. Later theorists in this tradition realized that, in a growing or changing economy, price level stability rather than deflation might be inconsistent with monetary neutrality, and (a postwar finding) that ex ante equality of savings and investment was an inadequate criterion for real equilibrium because neither was an operational magnitude; such equilibrium required equality of both with ex post investment and saving. The concern with preventing monetary developments from distorting real equilibrium rested on the assumption that, left to themselves, the real economic forces would tend to produce a welfare-optimizing equilibrium, an assumption that the Keynesian revolution effectively blasted, so that the concept of monetary equilibrium has now to be interpreted as a non-normative, purely positive, technique of analysis, as I understand it is in contemporary Dutch monetary theory. Moreover, recognition of the fact of economic growth destroyed the necessary equality of the real and money rates of interest — the relevant theory, which introduces expectations of the rate of price change as a wedge between the two, was provided by Irving Fisher but seems never to have made its way into European theorizing, whose efforts to cope with the problems of the interrelations among real growth, price trends, and interest rates remained groping. Thus my great teacher D.H. Robertson used to assert that the money price level should fall in proportion to the rate of increase of productivity, a proposition very similar to some modern results to be discussed later; but his argument rested on the desirability of enabling those retired from the active population to continue to share in the growth of productivity; through the resulting increase over time of the purchasing power of their annuities; and that argument was invalid, because it neglected the influence of the expected trend of prices on the money interest rates at which the retired would have accumulated their savings.

For what it was worth, however — and some of it was extremely subtle — monetary theory up into the 1930's suggested that the proper monetary policy would aim at a deflationary trend of prices related somehow to productivity growth. The contemporary popular emphasis on price stability as an objective of economic policy is a political simplification with no comparable theoretical justification. During the same period, however, some 'monetary heretics', including Keynes in the 1920's, had been developing an alternative view, namely that price inflation was good for prosperity and growth because it redistributed income from rentiers to entrepreneurs and so raised profits and stimulated investment. A further and related argument in the same vein, though one usually kept veiled in decent moral obscurity, is that inflation stimulates growth by redistributing income from workers to capitalists, with similar effects on investment. This view has its representatives among contemporary Keynesian growth theorists. But it involves the same basic theoretical flaw as its more orthodox contemporary, namely that it neglects the influence of price expectations on the determination of monetary rates of interest and of money wage rates. If inflation — or deflation, for that matter — comes to be anticipated with fair certainty on all sides, it should have no influence in redistributing income among the owners of factors of production, assuming that these owners behave rationally. (This does not deny that unexpected inflations or deflations do redistribute wealth between the holders and the issuers of fixed-interest securities.)

As already mentioned, the concern of monetary theorists up to the mid-1930's with monetary equilibrium, monetary neutrality, and the desirable trend of the price level was swept into limbo by the Keynesian Revolution, at least in English-language economics. Contemporary monetary theorists, however, have been returning to these problems in a somewhat different and more explicitly growth-oriented context, namely the role of money in models of economic growth and the somewhat misleadingly named problem of 'the optimum quantity of money'.[11] The essence of the problem as theoretically constructed is that money is assumed to cost nothing to produce and also to bear no explicit yield, but instead to bear an implicit negative or positive yield determined by the rate of inflation or deflation maintained by government monetary policy. The problem, then, is to choose the optimal rate of monetary growth and corresponding price trend, to maximize the community's welfare along an exogenously-determined growth path (the rate of growth in the long run being determined exogenously by the rates of growth of population and of labour-augmenting technical progress).

The answer is complicated if the economy is assumed to save irrationally according to a fixed savings ratio or desired wealth-to-income ratio, because then its consumption may fall short (on either side) of the technically maximum possible consumption per head, and if it falls short through insufficiency of capital per head (the more reasonable case) increasing capital stock and therefore consumption per head by manipulating the cost of money-holding and therefore the amount of saving that goes into material capital involves an intertemporal choice problem insoluble in terms of the model. If, on the other hand, saving can be assumed to be motivated by rational utility maximization, welfare maximization requires satiating the demand for real balances, which in turn requires deflating the economy's price level at a rate equal to the rate of return on material capital. In short, with much theoretical pyrotechnical display, contemporary pure monetary theory arrives at the same broad conclusion as the interwar style of monetary equilibrium theory, that optimality requires a deflationary trend of prices.

This conclusion, however, assumes that money is inherently non-interest-bearing, so that price deflation is required to endow it with the real yield necessary to satiate the demand for it (which demand by assumption is socially costless to satisfy). If, instead, it is assumed that in practice money is predominantly produced by a competitive banking system paying competitive interest rates on deposits — a situation which could be created by government policy where it does not now exist — the conclusion falls to the ground, because any rate of inflation maintained by the monetary authority would be reflected in money rates of interest on bank deposits as well as on other monetary assets and hence cause no distortions from the optimum quantity of money. The theoretical analysis would then have to turn to other considerations not currently allowed for, most obviously the relative economic costs of operating an economy with rising or falling prices as compared with stable prices. Such an analysis would probably lead to the common-sense conclusion that price stability is optimal in this respect and that inflation imposes additional welfare-reducing information and transactions costs. But the resulting loss from mild and not too erratic inflation on this account would probably be of a negligible order of magnitude, certainly not large enough to justify a strong policy of resistance to inflation.

NOTES

[1]   I am indebted to an unpublished monograph by Professor Frits de Jong, Developments of monetary theory in the Netherlands. Mimeographed, Department of Economics, Florida State University, Tallahassee, Florida, 1970. This gives an excellent account of the work of Dutch economists in this area. I am also indebted to a recent paper by Dr. M.W. Holtrop (On the effectiveness of monetary policy: The experience of the Netherlands in the years 1954-69. *The Journal of Money, Credit and Banking* (May 1972)) for an analysis of the monetary model of the Netherlands Bank and an evaluation of the performance of Dutch monetary policy based on it.

[2] On this see Axel Leijonhufvud's monumental study, *On Keynesian Economics and The Economics of Keynes*. London, Toronto, New York, Oxford University Press, 1968, and my review of it (Keynes and the Keynesians, *Encounter* 23,1 (January 1970) 70-73).

[3] I quote from memory of his lectures, though I have the impression that this characteristically sapient remark appears in at least one of his postwar II publications.

[4] See for example R.C.O. Matthews, Why has Britain had full employment since the war? *Economic Journal* 78, 311 (September 1968) 555-69.

[5] Nicholas Kaldor, The sea-change of the dollar, The new era of floating rates, and Reserves on a commodity standard, *The Times*, London, September 6, 7 and 8, 1971.

[6] M.W. Reder, The theoretical problems of a national wage-price policy, *Canadian Journal of Economics and Political Science* 14, 1 (February 1948) 46-61.

[7] J.R. Hicks, Economic foundations of wage policy, *Economic Journal* 66, 259 (September 1955) 388-404.

[8] For a refutation of this hypothesis in the context of Chilean experience, see Tom E. Davis, Eight decades of inflation in Chile: A political interpretation, *Journal of Political Economy* 71, 4 (August 1963) 389-97.

[9] See my Government and the corporation: A fallacious analogy, in: *Approaches to Greater Flexibility of Exchange Rates: The Burgenstock Papers*, George N. Halm, ed. (Princeton: Princeton University Press, 1970).

[10] Anthony Downs, *An Economic Theory of Democracy* (New York: Harper and Row, 1957).

[11] See particularly, James Tobin, Money and economic growth, *Econometrica* 33, 4 (October 1965) 671-84; Harry G. Johnson, Money

in a neo-classical one-sector growth model, ch. 4 in: *Essays in Monetary Economics* (London: Allen and Unwin, 1967); James Tobin, Notes on optimal monetary growth, *Journal of Political Economy* 76, 4, supplement (August 1968) 833-59; A.L. Marty, The optimal rate of growth of money, ibid., 860-73; Harry G. Johnson, Inside money, outside money, income, wealth and welfare in monetary theory, *Journal of Money, Credit and Banking* I, 1 (February 1969) 30-45; Miguel Sidrauski, Inflation and economic growth, *Journal of Political Economy* 75, 6 (December 1967) 796-810; D. Levhari and D. Patinkin, The role of money in a simple growth model, *American Economic Review* 58, 4 (September 1968) 713-53.

CHAPTER II

INFLATION THEORY
AND THE
MONETARIST CONTROVERSY

In my first lecture, I dealt with some general questions
regarding the causes and consequences of the inflationary tendencies that have been endemic in the
western capitalist world since the second world war,
and ended with a discussion of the economic costs of
inflation considered as a deterrent to the pursuit of
inflationary policies, and a brief survey of what the
recently-developed theory of the role of money in
growth models has to say about the economic consequences of inflation and the optimal price-trend for
monetary policy to pursue. The outcome of a great
deal of high-powered work, at least in my view, is a
strong case for stability of the trend of prices, rather
than the erratic, partly politically-determined, accel-
erations and decelerations that have been characteristic of most countries during the period; but a very

weak case indeed, and one that has to be based on considerations of transactions and calculation costs that have only recently begun to be introduced into monetary theory [1] , for the pursuit of a zero price trend (price stability) as a major goal of economic policy. In this lecture, I turn to the more narrowly professional economics question of the theory of inflation and of policies to control it. While I shall be primarily concerned with recent controversies in this area, I find it helpful to begin with a brief historical sketch of the development of monetary theory, with particular reference to the question of inflation, to give perspective on current issues.

For well over two thousand years, at least some men at at least some times and in some places have realized that inflation is the consequence of, or at least associated with, the excessive issue of money; and more generally, that trends in the general level of money prices are the consequences of, or at least associated with, movements in the relation between the supply of and the demand for the nominal stock of money. The intellectual expression of this understanding is the quantity theory of money, which reflects the on-going theoretical efforts of some of the finest minds humanity has produced. The list of contributors includes, in most nearly contemporary times, John Maynard Keynes — and not merely the Keynes of the *Tract* and the *Treatise*, but also the Keynes of the *General Theory*, even though the immediate impact of the *General Theory* in the eyes of the Keynesians — and mistakenly — was apparently to destroy the quantity theory once and for all.

Unfortunately, the construction of an adequate quantity theory of monetary phenomena, meeting the requirements on the one hand of intellectual elegance and consistency with economic theory in general, and on the other of practical applicability to relevant problems, is an extremely formidable intellectual task. The problem of constructing an adequate theory of relative prices to the same specifications is far easier — though even with respect to that task it has taken well into contemporary times (the postwar II period) for the generality of economists to become familiar with and accustomed to using the concepts of general rather than partial equilibrium. Correspondingly, there have always been strong pressures on the generality of economists, especially those most immediately concerned with practical affairs and policy problems, to backslide into attempts to explain monetary phenomena by relative price theory, supplemented by ad hoc fragments of monetary analysis derived from casual observation. This tendency, as I hope to show later in this lecture, has been particularly characteristic of postwar II theorizing about the causes of inflation and the design of policies to deal with it.

The intellectual difficulties in the formulation of an adequate quantity theory just mentioned begin with the problem of explaining the reasons for the emergence of a money economy from the barter economy, and determining the essential distinguishing functions of money in such an economy. The tradition has been to assume the existence of a monetary economy, and then to discern the functions of money within it by a process of essentially circular reasoning, Monetary theorists have only very recently become concerned with this basic question: as Karl Brunner has recently argued, in one of the best available statements of the emerging approach, which runs in terms of the information costs of transacting exchanges[2], both Keynesian theory and the neo-quantity theory of contemporary times commence their analyses by this essentially circular procedure. The by-passing of this basic issue is largely, though in some ways rather indirectly, responsible for the major divisions that have run through the history of the evolution of monetary theory more or less up to the present. One such is the division, now pretty well disposed of by the postwar II reformulation of the quantity theory as a theory of demand for money in capital—theoretic terms, between the Fisherine approach to quantity theory in terms of the equation $MV = PT$, which directed attention to the role of money as medium of exchange and to the 'objective' institutional determinants of the velocity of circulation, and the 'Cambridge'—Walrasian approach in terms of the equation $M = kOP$, which directed attention to the 'subjective' factors determining the desired ratio of cash balances to income and in so doing introduced, at least in a rudimentary way on which more recent theory (both Keynesian and quantity) has been able to build, the notion of money-holding as one alternative form of wealth-holding.

Another and more important issue concerns the institutional nature of money, an apparently simple and obvious empirical question which nevertheless poses the important theoretical question of how to formulate the mechanics of the influence running from monetary changes to price changes. The literature, as Arthur Marget documented in excessive detail in his monumental study[3], and as is familiar from contemporary debate, contains two rival versions of these mechanics, cash-balance mechanics and interest-rate or savings—investment or income—expenditure mechanics, corresponding broadly to the alternative assumptions that money is a commodity — as it was through most of the nineteenth century — and hence changes in its quantity change wealth, and that money is a double-entry-book-keeping credit creation — as it increasingly became towards the end of the nineteenth century — so that changes in its quantity change only the composition of wealth.

The difficulty of reconciling the cash-balance mechanics of traditional quantity theory with the apparent facts of life in a credit money system has remained to the present a key argument of the opponents of the quantity theory, who find more common sense in a naive income—expenditure approach to the explanation of monetary developments, and has also persistently troubled quantity theorists, who have had to construct transparently artificial examples such as a showering of bank notes on the public through their letter-boxes or via helicopter in order to explain their theory.

It led Wicksell to his brilliant switch of assumptions about the institutional nature of money to a pure credit system and a corresponding interest-rate savings–investment account of the mechanics of monetary disturbance, an innovation followed by Keynes. Unfortunately for the subsequent development of monetary theory, the combined effect of the challenge to the Keynesian assertion of the possibility of under-employment equilibrium with wage–price flexibility based on 'the Pigou effect', and the limitations of the mathematics of Walrasian general equilibrium theory, which more or less force the theorist into treating money as a commodity, forced monetary theory in the postwar II period, as represented by Don Patinkin's monumental work *Money, Interest and Prices*[4], back into the initial classical framework of formulating monetary theory on the basis of a commodity money. This formulation could only be justified by redefining 'money' to coincide with government debts to the public, and assuming as an empirical fact without real theoretical justification that the public regards its holding of its debts to itself through its government as net wealth. This extremely artificial foundation for monetary theory in turn provided the opportunity for Gurley and Shaw's reworking of monetary theory in terms of the distinction between 'inside' and 'outside' money[5], and the subsequent assault on this distinction by Pesek and Saving[6], who rightly demonstrated that inside money that bears no yield constitutes net wealth to the community just like outside money, but then wrongly — in my opinion and that of most other monetary theorists — attempted to assert that money must be of this non-interest-bearing nature to be money, and hence by implication that monetary theory must be formulated in terms of the traditional cash-balance mechanics.

A second fundamental source of difficulty in the formulation of a satisfactory quantity theory of money arises from the limitations of the conceptual tools available to economists at any time, and hence of the question they find it relevant or interesting to ask. A proper formulation requires a sophisticated understanding of the relation of wealth and income concepts and of the relation between stock and flow adjustments; in short, on elaboration of capital theory suitable for the analysis of disequilibrium situations. The traditional cash-balance mechanics provided a very crude and increasingly implausible version of it by condensing what were essentially stock adjustments into expenditure flows. It took the long-neglected work of Irving Fisher on the relation between capital and income (and on the dynamic influence of price expectations or the relation between real and money interest rates), together with Keynes's challenging formulation of the role of V or K as a problem of explaining the demand for money as a demand for a particular form of wealth, to set contemporary monetary theory on the proper track towards an adequate formulation.[7]

Again, it is understandable that the classical and neo-classical economists, having put so much effort into the discovery and elaboration of the fact that the real economic system is a system organized by the principle of maximization under competition, and limited initially by lack of mathematics and subsequently by the limitations of the calculus to static maximization problems, should have been primarily concerned with the proposition that money is merely a veil over the workings of the real (barter) economy, should have concentrated their monetary analysis on the vaguely-defined long run in which full employment of resources could be assumed, and should have settled on the question of the requirements for monetary equilibrium or monetary neutrality as their line of approach to the analysis of monetary disturbances and monetary dynamics — an approach very similar to the earlier classical approach to market dynamics in terms of the concept of 'normal price'. This orientation towards the conveniently long run, however, left the intellectual tradition they established unable to cope satisfactorily with the causes and dynamics of shorter-run monetary disturbances, and obliged to resort to ad hoc explanations in terms either of essentially inexplicable variations in variables assumed to be stable in the longer-run analysis, notably the velocity of circulation and the level of output, or even more confused and confusing, of real developments over

42

which by the longer-run theory money merely cast a veil — hence among other things the attempts of some contemporary monetary theorists to explain the great depression of the 1930's in terms of a presumed satiation of wants for goods and services.

It was this weakness — and in some cases disinterest in, disdain for, or incomprehension of the problem — on the part of quantity theory as it existed in the 1920's with respect to the problem of short-run disturbances that offered the point of attack on orthodoxy and the opportunity for success of the Keynesian revolution. Keynes, using the new concept of the multiplier, the absence of which had made previous attempts to explain business cycles and depressions logically unsatisfactory, was able to present a theoretically appealing explanation of short-run fluctuations in employment and output to fill the obvious gap in received monetary theory, albeit both the tradition of monetary theory and the polemical prerequisites of intellectual victory required him to cast the new theory in terms of a theory of employment equilibrium of which classical full employment was a mere special case. Moreover, the simplicity of his income—expenditure mechanics and the complexity of his monetary theory attracted many followers who were only too happy to dismiss the monetary theory — and all monetary theory — as irrelevant and accept the income—expenditure, real theory, side of the model as constituting the essential revolution. This position is a major example of the temptation to intellectual backsliding mentioned earlier; it remains characteristic of the Keynesian tradition in theory, though obviously not of the more eminent Keynesian monetary theorists, and is the focal point of the monetarist controversy to be discussed later in this lecture. It is on the other hand a characteristic reflection of the strength of orthodox tradition in economic theory that the challenge of Keynesian theory, which as mentioned was essentially concerned with changing the perspective of monetary theory from long-run equilibrium to short-run disequilibrium analysis, was met by rapidly shifting the debate back to the realm of long-run full-employment equilibrium, and focussing on the questions of the "neutrality" of money and the validity or otherwise of the "classical dichotomy" between value theory and monetary theory, issues posed by the classical concern with money as a veil over the barter system, overlooking even the neo-classical concern with the requirements of monetary neutrality; and that quantity theorists have only recently turned to the central Keynesian problem of short-run monetary dynamics.

Primarily because of the intellectual difficulty of monetary theory, allied with the preference of economists as human beings for relying on their own concepts of common sense in understanding the world in which they live, there has always been a strong current of scepticism about and opposition to the basic proposition of the quantity theory, that the demand for and supply of money play an important part in monetary developments and disturbances. The ideas involved are fairly obvious and of long standing, as are the answers to them, but this has not prevented them from turning up persistently as novel discoveries of the would-be anti-orthodox, sometimes but not characteristically with some pretensions to superior sophistication of the objection at issue. Most of them have been newly discovered in recent controversy by the opponents of monetarism. A basic thread linking them together, I will remark without elaborating on the point, is an elementary confusion between nominal money and real money, and a failure to realize that, in contrast to the real demand and supply factors that govern the real quantities of goods and services produced and consumed, the real stock of money is determined, eventually at least, by the behaviour of the public in determining the money price level. This elementary confusion leads to a tendency to discuss monetary problems as if nominal and real money balances are the same thing, and as if ordinary value theory could be applied to the behaviour of money.[8]

In dealing in a preliminary fashion with these standard objections to the quantity theory, it is convenient to recall a remark once made by Gottfried Haberler, to the effect that there is no proposition in economics so patently stupid that an apparently very similar proposition cannot be found that can be plausibly defended intellectually.[9] One must be extremely wary of the half-truth and the true but irrelevant proposition. The objection in question can be put sequentially, in terms of a crude but I believe generally acceptable version of the mechanism of transmission of monetary impulses to the economy.

The first objection is that the monetary authority cannot control the money supply. This objection, which harks back to the controversy between the Currency School and the Banking School in the early nineteenth century, is obviously and patently at variance with the long-established theory and practice of central banking. The parallel half-truth is that the control of the money supply is not as tight as some mechanical models of money supply determination have implied, because the connection between monetary policy actions and the money supply runs through behaviour relations on the part of the public and the banks (and perhaps other financial institutions depending on the institutional definition of money employed). But this does not destroy the possibility of control so long as the relevant behaviour relationships are stable and predictable, as observation and empirical research suggest they are. A theoretically irrelevant truth is that if the monetary authority chooses not to control the money supply, but instead for example attempts to fix the level of interest rates, the money supply will be a dependent and not a controlled variable.Such central bank behaviour has been an important fact of life since the second world war, with the dominance over monetary policy achieved by the interests of Treasuries in holding down interest rates on the public debt and maintaining 'orderly market conditions' for such debt. But it does not constitute a refutation of the quantity theory; on the contrary, its theoretically predictable consequences in producing both inflation and rising money interest rates constitute an important validation of the quantity theory. Another truth, which is theoretically irrelevant to the debate in its usual context of a closed economy but highly relevant to the theory and conduct of monetary policy in an open economy — as will be seen in my next lecture — is that in an open economy the money supply is in the long run endogenous and not exogenous, because the public can import or export nominal money through the balance of payments and so adjust the money supply to what it wants to hold, by a mechanism alternative to the classical quantity theory's adjustment of actual to desired real balances through movements of the price level in face of a policy-determined nominal stock of money. This point carries the important implication that the monetary authority can only control the price level — specifically in the contemporary world, prevent inflation — if it is prepared to vary its exchange rate or let it float. But this implication derives from the quantity theory and is in no sense a refutation of it.

The second objection is that, though the monetary authority can control the money supply, it cannot thereby influence the economy, because, it is alleged, there is an almost infinite elasticity of substitution between money, on any of the conventional definitions of it, and money substitutes, which latter are in nearly perfectly elastic supply, so that the public will always be able to get the money it wants from some source, public or private. This objection originated in contemporary monetary theory as the Keynesian 'absolute liquidity trap' hypothesis, with bonds serving as perfect money-substitutes; it then, with somewhat more apparent plausibility, became the Radcliffe Report/Gurley and Shaw contention that money is merely the small change of the financial system and that financial intermediation makes the elasticity of demand for money extremely high. In this form the objection rests on an invalid transformation of theoretical possibilities into alleged facts, and also a confusion between money and credit. Again, so long as the substitution behaviour involved is reasonably stable and predictable, as both general reasoning and empirical evidence suggest that it is, the objection constitutes no refutation of the quantity theory.

The relevant half-truth is that an elaborate structure of financial intermediation may — not necessarily does — make the problem of monetary control more complex than simple monetary models assume. The irrelevant truth is that the financial system is indeed a complex structure.

The third objection is that, even though the monetary authorities can control the quantity of money, and even though near-money assets are not perfect substitutes for money, the changes in the terms of substitution between money and near money assets consequent on monetary policy changes have no or negligible effects on the 'real' side of the model, i.e. on expenditures on goods and services. This objection goes back to the dissatisfaction already mentioned with the 'cash-balance mechanics' of one variant of the quantity theory and the preference for the 'interest-rate' (or savings–investment) mechanics of the Wicksell–Keynes variant, and the post-Keynesian discovery that complete interest-inelasticity of the savings and investment functions of the simplified Keynesian general equilibrium model precludes a monetary effect on the real sector. It expresses itself in the contemporary debate over the quantity theory and monetarism in the claim that the quantity theory provides no satisfactory explanation of the mechanism whereby monetary impulses are transmitted to the real sector. This objection rests on the false methodological principle that theory must be both more naive than the reality it seeks to explain, and expressed in terms of the critic's personal and anti-scientific concepts of common-sense and satisfactory explanations. Moreover, it prejudges the issue by demanding an explanation in terms of a logical structure of causation adopted a priori and by its construction incapable of being satisfied on the issue. Specifically, there is no theoretical justification for assuming that the causal sequence must run from money to the yields on monetary assets to expenditure on a particular set of real assets distinguished conceptually and statistically as 'real investment', rather than from money to all assets held in the portfolio, both money and real, the latter including a great many items such as consumer durables not normally classed as investment and not carrying yields observable in the markets. Nor is it legitimate to insist that an acceptable explanation must prove a positive interest-rate effect on real investment or saving, when the theoretical model that arbitrarily makes this the test is arbitrarily set up precisely to emphasize the possibility that such an effect may be (even will normally be) absent. Despite the difficulties econometricians have had in finding empirical evidence of an interest-rate influence on real industrial investment, even with the aid of complex lagged capital-stock adjustment models, the evidence in my view is overwhelming that changes in the money stock do influence money expenditure. The half-truth that parallels the objection is that, under certain circumstances and for a significant time, monetary impulses may be largely diverted into changes in money holdings (hoarding or dishoarding); but no quantity theorist has ever denied this, and the great theorists of monetary equilibrium and neutrality were very concerned to emphasize that monetary management must recognize and avert the destabilizing consequences of changes in the public's desire to hold money. The irrelevant truth about the objection is that lazy minds would rather reiterate the list of all theoretical possibilities than weed some of them out by hard theoretical and empirical work, and that dogmatists would rather cavil forever than admit shortcomings in their understanding of economics requiring new thought on their part.

50

I have spent rather a long time on general issues in monetary theory, instead of on its specific application to inflation theory, in order to emphasize both that the issues in the contemporary debate over inflation are general issues of monetary theory, and that these issues have been around for well over a century and should not be interpreted as a new set of issues raised by a new and eccentric vocal minority espousing a new theory called monetarism. To return to the main theme of the lecture, the accepted theory of inflation and of anti-inflationary policy up until the Keynesian revolution was firmly based on the quantity theory of money. The Keynesian revolution, at least in the English-language countries, destroyed the intellectual credentials of that approach — which has only painfully and slowly been restored to academic respectability in the past fifteen years and especially the last five — and thus created a theoretical vacuum that had to be filled by new construction when inflation again became a problem during and after the second world war. (An honorable exception must be made for the Dutch tradition of monetary theory, which pragmatically digested Keynes's empirically useful division of the demand for money into a transactions component related to income and a liquidity component related to interest rates, and integrated it with the traditional approach to monetary analysis and stabilization policy based on the concept of monetary equilibrium.)

Initially, given the wartime resort to widespread wage and price controls, and to extensive physical rationing, the problem of inflation control was a relatively simple one for the new Keynesian theory to handle, since it required only the simple proposition that aggregate demand from all sources had to be constrained to aggregate supply capacities by taxation, rationing, shortages and queues enforced by price controls, and patriotic austerity in consumption. Once the controls began to come off and suppressed inflation to be replaced by open inflation, it was quickly discovered that plausible and appealing models of inflation could be patched together from ideas inherited from the 1930's. First, and most important, the Keynesian multiplier theory could readily be converted from a dynamic model of quantity changes in aggregate output in response to an initial exogenous shock of demand change, to a dynamic model of price level change in response to an exogenous change in real aggregate demand or supply potential in conditions of full employment. Second, the models could be enriched by drawing from imperfect competition theory the assumption that prices and wages could be either competitively demand-determined, or administratively cost-determined, thus introducing the distinction between demand-pull and cost-push inflation that has characterized both popular and professional discussions of the inflation problem ever since. Third, the models could be given political appeal and social verisimilitude by depicting the inflation process as a "struggle for income shares" between workers and capitalists, with the rentiers sometimes appearing as their joint victim and the source of mutual benefit from inflation. The game of model-construction on these lines acquired considerable impressiveness, and incidentally created a number of professional reputations, through the discovery of first-order and especially second-order difference equations, with their rich menu of possible patterns of dynamic behaviour. The main positive findings were that inflation would take place at a finite time-rate, and that it would either converge on a new equilibrium price level or accelerate, depending on whether one of the social groups contending for real income could be brought by the inflationary process to accept a lower income share than that originally asked for, or not.

Interest in these models — which were really no more than mechanical playthings for economists learning a new and to them difficult kind of mathematics — rapidly died out as the first postwar wave of inflation subsided. They were in any case very bad economic models. Not only did they completely ignore the monetary requirements of inflation, implicitly assuming either a vastly excessive existing stock of money or a permissively expansionary monetary policy of maintaining fixed and low interest rates; that assumption would have been empirically justified by the facts of the immediate postwar situation in the relevant countries, though it should have been made explicitly rather than incorporated implicitly in the models. They also ignored both the marginal productivity theory of distribution as a determinant of the feasible real equilibrium of the system, and the formation of expectations based on past experience as an influence on both wage and price determination and the length of the period separating successive adjustments of wages and prices. In consequence, they depended on the presence of money illusion on the part of some economic groups to explain both the dynamics of the inflationary process and its possible eventual termination — and while 'money illusion' is a justifiable short-hand description of economic behaviour based on confidence in the stability of the purchasing power of money in the face of short-run cyclical developments, it makes no theoretical sense as an assumption about behaviour in the face of a sustained unidirectional trend in the level of money prices.

Nevertheless, Keynesian theorizing about inflation, at least at the popular level that measures the heights to which the average professionally trained economist is capable of ascending, has moved very little beyond the rather naive and ad hoc ideas on which the early postwar Keynesian analyses were based. These, in a very brief sketch, are, first, that inflation is generally due to excess demand on productive capacity, though it may on occasion be due to 'excessive' claims for real income by particular groups of workers or capitalists, implemented by inflationary wage demands (assumed to be unchecked by employer resistance) or by inflationary price increases (assumed to be unchecked by consumer resistance). This idea involves the commonplace distinction between 'demand-pull' and 'cost-push' inflation, which in technical terms attributes inflation to the budget constraint of value theory being irrelevant either because it exceeds the community's capacity to produce, or because it becomes inoperative in the presence of monopoly power – the latter constituting elementary economic nonsense, though infinitely appealing to adherents of the naive political 'liberalism' developed in the 1930's of the 'New Deal' and the theory of imperfect competition.

In cases of 'demand-pull' inflation, the standard and obvious Keynesian policy recommendation is to cut aggregate demand down to the dimensions of aggregate supply by fiscal policy restraints. Monetary policy is presumed useful only to the extent that higher interest rates and credit rationing of various kinds by the banking system can effectively cut aggregate spending, with the further presumption that interest rates have little effect on aggregate demand while credit rationing has much. The monetarist position is of course almost the exact opposite: fiscal restraint can have little effect unless allied with monetary restraint, higher observed interest rates are the incidental by-products rather than the modus operandi of monetary restraint, and credit rationing in the absence of overall monetary restraint merely distorts resource allocation without being effective in reducing aggregate demand. These propositions are, naturally, empirical approximations; and they rest on the fundamental assumption that a highly developed

financial system permits a high degree of substitutability of one type of expenditure for another and one
source of finance for another, the ultimate constraint
on expenditure being the stock of money on which
the pyramidal structure of credit-creation rests.

With respect to 'cost-push' inflation, the obvious
policy recommendation for people naive enough to
accept the concept in the first place is the equally
naive proposal to stop the pushing, either by appealing
to the pushers' sense of decency or if necessary by
subjecting them to social discipline. The intellectual
flowering of this primitive appeal for the flouting of
economic laws by social conventions and constraints
appears in the solemn recommendation by authori-
tative economists of the need for an incomes policy.
As suggested earlier, an incomes policy involves the
self-contradicting aims of achieving an ethically-
dictated alteration of the distribution of real income
produced by economic forces, and of achieving the
economically-determined distribution of real income
without price inflation by piercing the veil of money.
It is an ironical paradox that Keynesian economics,
having begun with a head-on attack on the alleged
classical fallacy that money is merely a veil over the
workings of a barter economy, should have wound up
with the attempt to persuade the public that money is
in fact merely a veil, and that society should not only
recognize this but revert to the economics of barter —
or even revert still further to the feudal notion of the
'just-price' — and reduce money to the role of a pure

numéraire. Again, the quantity-theoretic or monetarist approach takes a diametrically opposite position to the Keynesian position. On that approach, 'cost-push' is merely an institutional manifestation of the natural tendency to restore equilibrium real relative price relatonships whose expression in monetary terms has been disrupted by the erosion of the real value of money through inflation, and an incomes policy can only succeed if it is backed up by sufficient monetary restraint to make stability of money prices on the average, and the corresponding behaviour of money wages, rational behaviour in real terms for the individual economic decision-taking units concerned. Otherwise, the quantity theory approach predicts, with a degree of confidence amply justified by over a quarter of a century of experience and empirical research, that incomes policy, even if successful in its own terms, will have only the nuisance effect of fixing the nominal monetary label attached to transactions whose real dimensions are infinitely variable. On the side of commodity transactions, the resulting adjustments of contract terms are familiar in such phenomena as product adulteration, the introduction of new brand names with higher nominal price-tags, the tying of sales of under-priced items to purchases of over-priced items, and the development of queueing, under-the-counter sales, and other devices for preventing consumers from shopping around and so reducing inventory-holding costs for retailers and suppliers. On the side of labour-market transactions, the adjustment of real contract terms to the constraint of fixed nominal price tags is equally familiar, in such phenomena as the up-grading of labour skill classifications, the relaxation of discrimination against women, juveniles, and ethnic or religious minority groups, and the provision of additional non-wage-rate real income in the form of guaranteed bonus-rate overtime hours, pensions and other non-work-related fringe benefits, and free or subsidized lunches and other conventionally non-recorded income in kind.

The evolution of Keynesian theory since the immediate postwar period has in fact produced only one significant contribution to monetary analysis — the Phillips curve, relating the rate of wage inflation to the level of unemployment.[10, 11] And that contribution, besides being merely a contribution to empirical understanding of the mechanics of the inflationary process rather than to theoretical understanding of the causes and policy implications of inflation, and despite the limitless possibilities of empirical and theoretical elaboration that it created, has become increasingly suspect. In the first place, ever since its invention there has been good reason for statistically theoretical doubt whether the curvilinear regression form that created and validated the empirical relationship represented a true empirical economic law (like the Engel curve and the Pareto law of distribution), or a statistical artifact that linked together two quite incomparable behavioural situations: full employment, and unexpectedly large-scale unemployment produced by economic depression. In the second place, the theory behind the Phillips curve represents about the crudest and least sophisticated possible economic explanation of the dynamics of economic markets, in two related senses. First, it assumes that the dynamics of market price adjustment are dominated by realized excess demand or supply in that particular market, virtually regardless of developments in other markets; and second, it assumes for this purpose that money price adjustments and real relative price adjustments are identical and comprehensible in a single theory. In other and shorter words, the theory of the Phillips curve not only derives intellectually from a Hicks–Patinkin type of model with a constant nominal quantity of money, but simplifies that model for mathematical convenience into one in which price movements in a particular market are derived solely from the excess demand/excess supply position in that market. In the third place, of much less scientific but much more practical importance, the Phillips curve approach to inflation policy seems to have broken down completely in the face of the inflationary facts of the past two years or so, in the sense that the major countries (especially the United Kingdom and the United States) have had both faster inflation and more unemployment than previous empirical work on the Phillips curve suggested was empirically possible. This fact, however, has been embarrassingly inexplicable not only for Keynesian theory — which has been torn between the alternative scientifically unsatisfactory

59

hypotheses that the Phillips curve has collapsed completely, and that it has merely shifted outwards for some unpredictable exogenous reason — but also for the monetarist approach, which has gained much of its recently-restored popularity from the confident allegation that it comprehended the phenomena of inflation much more adequately in scientific terms than the rival Keynesian approach.

This point brings me to the postwar II revival of the quantity theory approach, or 'the rise of monetarism', as it has come to be called in recent years. This revival has been largely the work of my Chicago colleague Milton Friedman and his students, though in recent years the mantle of leadership has increasingly passed to Karl Brunner and Allan Meltzer, a team originally formed at the University of California, Los Angeles, and whose work has been strongly influenced (as has that of Axel Leijonhufvud) by the ideas of a Chicago graduate of an earlier generation, Armen Alchian — ideas that stress the concept of information and transactions costs. I have dealt with the revival and successful diffusion of the modernized quantity theory approach on a number of recent occasions[1][2], and will deal with the earlier stages of it in only the briefest of detail here. The starting point was a restatement of the quantity theory of money as a capital-theoretic formulation of the demand for money, absorbing the best ideas of Keynes and Irving Fisher, and involving neither of the two assumptions that had been the gravamen of Keynesian ridiculing of previous versions of the theory — the assumptions that the economy naturally tends towards the condition of full employment, which was declared to be a matter of supply response not properly belonging to monetary theory, and that the velocity of circulation is a parametric constant subject to arbitrary variations, which was replaced by the assertion that velocity is a behavioural functional relationship of a few variables that have to be appropriately measured.[13] The next step was the empirical testing of the quantity theory so reformulated against the rival Keynesian theory, which for this purpose was identified in terms of Friedman's methodology of positive economics with the simple theory of the multiplier.[14] The methodological foundations of the tests, which were strongly at variance with the general predilection of contemporary economists for the construction of macro-economic general equilibrium systems of equations rather than single-equation reduced forms emphasizing one causal relationship, both guaranteed the victory of the quantity theory over the Keynesian in terms of the chosen test procedure and thoroughly confused and confounded the Keynesian opposition, which instead of ridiculing and dismissing the methodology attempted to prove that despite its ridiculousness it yielded results favouring Keynesianism when properly interpreted and applied — and so fell into a series of traps laid by the unfamiliarity of the methodological ground-rules.[15]

The third step in the restoration of respectability to the quantity theory was the use of Friedman's 1968

Presidential Address to the American Economic Association[16] to state in simple and logical terms the essence of the quantity theory critique of the prevailing Keynesian views on the use of policy, in the form of the strong (and long-run) proposition that monetary policy can control monetary magnitudes — specifically the price level, and through the influence of expectations about the rate of inflation the level of money interest rates in relation to the real rate of interest — but not real magnitudes such as the level of unemployment or the rate of economic growth, which are determined by the real forces operating in the economy.

Despite these academic, scholarly-intellectual developments, however, the real motive force behind the rise of 'monetarism' (the quantity theory approach) in popular thinking in recent years has been the failure of the alternative Keynesian approach to deal effectively with the problem of inflation in concrete economic-policy-making terms. In the United States, the issue centred around the fiscal policy emphasis of the 'new economics' of Walter Heller as Chairman of the Council of Economic Advisers during the Kennedy and Johnson Administrations, and most specifically the failure of the tax surcharge of 1968 to halt the inflation induced by the Johnson Administration's failure to finance the war in Vietnam by taxation, the failure of the surcharge being attributable to the policy of monetary expansion pursued by the Federal Reserve. In the United Kingdom, the switch of policy thinking to monetarism, which has most recently produced a major change in the operational methods of the Bank of England towards quantitative control of the money supply and away from the interest rate and credit control methods indicated by the philosophy of the Radcliffe Report and resorted to increasingly in the 1960's[1][7], has been fairly clearly attributable to the failure of the devaluation of 1967 both to produce the immediate balance-of-payments improvement predicted by the Keynesian theories applied to the analysis of its quantitative effects, and to succeed without the wage-and-price-inflationary consequences predicted by its critics. As an amateur judge of the competence of the performance of average professional opinion in various countries, I would opine, without justifying the judgment, that the sophistication of understanding of the American Keynesians was seriously under-estimated by their opponents — since by that time the best of them had remembered that the Keynesian system includes a monetary sector — while the English Keynesians on the contrary were even more scientifically illiterate in private than they appeared in public. Be that as it may, the triumph of monetarism has been short-lived in both countries, and the quantity-theoretic approach is again in popular eclipse, partly because in the euphoria of belated popular recognition the monetarists vastly exaggerated the potency — a different matter from the necessity — of monetary restraint as a means of stopping inflation once inflation is well under way, in terms of both the amount and the duration of the unemployment required to change inflationary expectations and therefore wage and price determination behaviour. In my own judgment, the recent reversal of anti-inflationary monetary policies reflects, not the mistakenness of the quantity theory, but the fact discussed in my first lecture that when the chips are down the political process attaches a relatively low cost to inflation and a relatively high cost to heavy unemployment.

Meanwhile, the temporary popularity of monetarism has naturally evoked in the sphere of academic scholarship a counter-attack by the Keynesians. In the United Kingdom, where the pseudo-scientific methodology of interpreting old facts and inventing new ones to support brightly unorthodox theories unfortunately prevails over the scientific methodology of determining the facts first and then testing theories against them, the counter-attack has consisted largely of pontifical rehearsal in modern jargon of the traditional and fallacious objections to the quantity theory.[18] In the United States, on the other hand, the debate has been fruitful and promises further scientific advance. Let me conclude this lecture by reporting three pointers towards future theoretical and empirical developments.

First, Leonall C. Andersen and his co-workers at the Federal Reserve Bank of St. Louis have taken over from Friedman–Meiselman the task of empirical exploration of the role of money in determining the development of money income, prices and output

64

over time.[19] In the course of their work, the emphasis has shifted from the starting point of testing the rival Keynesian and quantity theories against one another to the more policy-relevant practical question of the relative strength and reliability of monetary and fiscal policy changes as policy instruments; it has also become increasingly concerned with the practically important question, left open (deliberately) by Friedman's restatement of the quantity theory, of how the effect of a monetary impulse is divided between price level changes and output quantity changes. The upshot of this work in general has been to establish that relatively small-scale models emphasizing monetary forces are more efficient as economic predicters than the multi-equation models favoured by the Keynesian income—expenditure approach. This should prove comforting to the Dutch tradition of monetary analysis, which has consistently relied on models of this simple type.

Secondly, the Friedman criticism of the Phillips curve for ignoring the influence of expectations about future price trends in the determination of money wages has led to a much more thoughtful re-examination of the Phillips curve's theoretical foundations and empirical validity.[20] The most recent empirical finding, for the United States, is that wage determination is influenced by price expectations, contrary to the original formulation of the relationship, but that this influence is only partial, so that a modified version of the Phillips curve exists empirically, though it is far

65

less favourable than the original one to the idea of a 'policy trade-off' between inflation and unemployment. This finding, however, is not very satisfactory, either theoretically or empirically, and new work on the problem is likely to involve broadening the micro-economic foundations of the relationship in terms of the influence of information and adjustment costs and other real factors.[21]

Finally, recent work by both Keynesians and monetarists who have taken monetarism seriously has tended to show that, while monetary influences are indisputably important, the particular formulation of the monetarist position embodied in the past works of Milton Friedman is not in fact tolerably consistent with the empirical evidence; and this irt my judgment will prove to be an intellectually liberating discovery. Empirical work some time ago showed conclusively that, contrary to the evidence adduced by Friedman, the demand for money is a function of the rate of interest — as Keynes claimed and as Friedman's own theory in fact predicts should be the case. More recently, Tobin has demonstrated conclusively that the facts of monetary experience over the business cycle are more consistent with a properly sophisticated Keynesian theory than with Friedman's own version of the quantity theory.[22] Moreover, at the level of abstract monetary theory, Friedman has recently attempted to fill the gap in the empirical applicability of the quantity theory left by his restatement of that theory as a theory of demand for money, with no implications as to the relative magnitudes of the effects of monetary impulses on money prices and real quantities of output[23], with results that in my judgment come very close to returning monetary theory to the position reached in Franco Modigliani's classic article of 1944.[24] Friedman's theoretical efforts to restore the quantity theory to empirical relevance to practical policy problems will be the subject of a forthcoming highly critical symposium of leading monetary theorists in *The Journal of Political Economy*. The results, or at least so one hopes, should be to free both Keynesians and Friedmanians from the obligations of loyalty to what they believe to have been their master's words — though I would be the first to argue that in each case the master has displayed a far more subtle understanding of the provisional and temporally-oriented nature of the findings of scientific enquiry than his disciples have proved capable of comprehending — and to permit monetary theorists to concentrate the full range of diverse individual insights into monetary phenomena on the understanding of the pressing problems that confront us — which concern the short-run dynamics of an economic system in which money has an undeniable long-run determining influence.

NOTES

[1] See Axel Leijonhufvud, *On Keynesian Economics and the Economics of Keynes* (London, Toronto, New York: Oxford University Press, 1968), Ch. 1, and Karl Brunner, A survey of selected issues in monetary theory, *Schweizerische Zeitschrift für Volkswirtschaft und Statistik* 107th year, no. 1 (1971) 1-146, especially ch. 1.

[2] Karl Brunner, op. cit.

[3] Arthur W. Marget, *The Theory of Prices* (New York: Prentice-Hall, Vol. I, 1938, Vol. II, 1942).

[4] Don Patinkin, *Money, Interest and Prices* (Evanston: Row, Peterson, 1957; second edition New York: Harper and Row, 1965).

[5] J.G. Gurley and E.S. Shaw, *Money in a Theory of Finance* (Washington: The Brookings Institution, 1960).

[6] Boris P. Pesek and Thomas R. Saving, *Money, Wealth and Economic Theory* (New York: Macmillan, 1967).

[7] It must be noted, however, that recognition that this was what the 'Keynesian Revolution' had really done to advance monetary theory was long delayed by Keynes's inclusion of the traditional quantity theory as only one – and a minor – element in his theory of demand for money (the transactions motive) and his concentration on the speculative motive – gambling on expectations about short-run movements of bond prices – in explaining the demand for money as a form of wealth. In an important sense, Milton Friedman's restatement of the quantity theory of money (The quantity theory of money – A restatement, pp. 3-21 in: *Studies in the Quantity Theory of Money*, M. Friedman, ed., Chicago: University of Chicago Press, 1956) is a much clearer and more enlightening statement of Keynes's essential contribution to the development of monetary theory than the statements of Keynes and his followers.

[8] It should also be remarked that the most sophisticated of contemporary Keynesian monetary theorists, notably the Yale Group led by James Tobin, are obviously alert to this confusion but by-pass it

either by assuming stable prices and confining their analysis to the financial sector, or by building models based on the fictional construction of a money whose purchasing power is fixed in real terms, thereby avoiding confusion in the analysis at the expense of creating it with respect to the applicability of the results. See James Tobin, Commercial banks as creators of money, in: *Banking and Monetary Studies*, Deane Carson, ed. (Homewood, Illinois: Richard D. Irwin, 1963) and idem, Money and economic growth, *Econometrica* 33, 4 (October 1965), 67-86.

[9]   Again I quote from memory.

[10]   A. W. Phillips, The relationship between unemployment and the rate of change of money wage rates in the United Kingdom, 1861-1957, *Economica*, New Series, 25, 100 (November 1958) 283-99, and R.G. Lipsey, The relationship between unemployment and the rate of change of money wage rates in the United Kingdom, 1861-1957: A further analysis, *Economica*, New Series 27, 105 (February 1960) 1-31.

The subsequent literature is too voluminous to be worth recording, especially now that the American Economic Association is producing a regular and comprehensive bibliographical documentary record of the English-language literature.

[11]   One could add that Keynesian theory has also produced only one important contribution to general economic theory since the second world war. This was Roy Harrod's recognition (*Towards a Dynamic Economics*, London: Macmillan, 1948) that in addition to the short-run Keynesian problem of whether investment will absorb the saving that income-recipients would like to undertake at full-employment income levels, there is a long-run problem of whether the investment satisfactory to entrepreneurs will grow rapidly enough to maintain full employment of labour in the face of the natural growth of population and the presence of labour-saving technical progress. The Keynesian side of professional analysis of this question has degenerated rapidly into one of two forms, typified by the work of Keynes's successors at Cambridge. On the one hand there has been the effort, typified by Joan Robinson (*The Accumulation of Capital*, London: Macmillan, 1956) to show by proving fundamental logical flaws in the pure theory of capital that the capitalist system cannot possibly work, regardless of any empirical evidence to the contrary. On the other hand there has been acceptance of the fact that

69

capitalism has in fact worked fairly well during most of its history, and especially in the postwar period, coupled with the effort to prove that the reason cannot be that traditional theories of capitalism were in fact right, but that instead the reason must be found in new and equally unorthodox extensions of Keynesian theory designated to make good the alleged inadequacy of classical theory (see Nicholas Kaldor, *Essays in Economic Stability and Growth*, Glencoe, Illinois: The Free Press, 1960, especially Part III). My one-time professor in the history of economic thought, Joseph Schumpeter, used to tell us at Harvard (again I quote from memory) that when an economist made an empirical prediction that turned out to be completely wrong, he never said 'I am a fool! '; instead he said, 'Reality is even more complicated than I thought! ' The idea that it takes still more Keynesian theorizing to explain the failure of the original Keynesian theorizing is only, in one of Alfred Marshall's favourite phrases, 'a leading species of a large genus'.

The orthodox conservative side of the debate, however, which has been centred in Cambridge, Massachusetts, in the persons of Paul Samuelson and Robert Solow, has been equally quick to assume away the scientific relevance of Harrod's extension of the original Keynesian question by constructing models of economic growth that simply assume the maintenance of continuous full employment by a perfectly functioning system of market competition.

It has been extremely unfortunate for the progress of economic science that the two Cambridges have not only neutralized each other in a sterile and essentially ideological debate — a cost characteristic of most scientific advances — but that their feuding has diverted so many young economists into the belief that heroism in this sham battle would advance the cause of economic understanding. As a result, recognizable progress in monetary theory has had to depend on scholars associated neither directly nor indirectly with these institutions of higher learning. (For fear of misunderstanding, I should record that I include in this group of contributions the important work on the development of liquidity preference theory and the analysis of the financial sector pursued at Yale University under the leadership of James Tobin.)

[12] Harry G. Johnson, Monetary theory and policy, *American Economic Review* LII, 3 (June 1962) 335-84. Reprinted as Ch. I in *Essays in Monetary Theory* (London: Allen and Unwin, 1967); Recent

developments in monetary theory: A commentary, in: *Money in Britain, 1959-1969*, D. Croome and H.G. Johnson (eds.), (Oxford: The Clarendon Press, 1970) 83-114; The Keynesian revolution and the monetarist counter-revolution, *The American Economic Review* 61, 2 (May 1971) 1-14.

[13] Milton Friedman, The quantity theory of money – A restatement, *Studies in the Quantity Theory of Money* (Chicago: University of Chicago Press, 1956), 3-21, and, The demand for money: Some theoretical and empirical results, *The Journal of Political Economy* 67, 4 (August 1959), 327-51.

[14] Milton Friedman and Gary S. Backer, A statistical illusion in judging Keynesian models, *Journal of Political Economy* 65, 1 (February 1957) 64-75; Milton Friedman and David Meiselman, The relative stability of monetary velocity and the investment multiplier in the United States, 1898-1958, in: Commission on Money and Credit *Stabilization Policies* (Englewood Cliffs, N.J.: Prentice-Hall, 1963) 165-268. For the controversy on the former, see John Johnston, A statistical illusion in judging Keynesian models: Comment, *Review of Economics and Statistics* 40 (August 1958) 296-98; Edwin Kuh, A note on prediction from Keynesian models, *Review of Economics and Statistics* 40 (August 1958) 294-95; M. Friedman and Gary S. Becker, Reply to Kuh and Johnston, *Review of Economics and Statistics* 40 (August 1958) 298; and Milton Friedman and Gary S. Becker, The Friedman–Becker Illusion: Reply, Journal of Political Economy 66 (December 1958) 545-49. For references to the controversy on the latter, see footnote 15.

[15] Donald D. Hester, Keynes and the quantity theory: A comment on the Friedman–Meiselman CMC paper, and M. Friedman and D. Meiselman, Reply to Donald Hester, *Review of Economics and Statistics* 46, 4 (November 1964) 364-68 and 369-76; Albert Ando and Franco Modigliani, Velocity and the investment multiplier; Michael de Prano and Thomas Mayer, Autonomous expenditure and money; Milton Friedman and David Meiselman, Reply; and other authors' Rejoinders, *American Economic Review* 55, 4 (September 1965) 693-728, 729-52, 753-85, 786-90, 791-92. For a subsequent commentary on the issues, see Stephanie K. Edge, The relative stability of velocity and the invest-

ment multiplier, *Australian Economic Papers* 6, 9 (December 1967) 192-207. The appropriately effective scientific Keynesian rejoinder of disputing the methodology of the test rather than the test results themselves was adopted by P.A. Samuelson (Problems of methodology – Discussion, *American Economic Review* 53, 2 (May 1963) 231-36) but without significant immediate impact on the course of the controversy in monetary theory.

16 Milton Friedman, The role of monetary policy, *American Economic Review* 57, 1 (March 1968) 1-17.

17 For the background to this change, see D.R. Croome and Harry G. Johnson, *Money in Britain, 1959–1969* (Oxford: Oxford University Press, 1970).

18 See in particular Nicholas Kaldor, The New Monetarism, *Lloyds Bank Review* 97 (July 1970) 1-18; Milton Friedman, Comment, and Nicholas Kaldor, Reply, *Lloyds Bank Review* 98 (October 1970) 52-53, and 54-55.

19 Leonall C. Andersen and Jerry L. Jordan, Monetary and fiscal actions: A test of their relative importance in economic stabilization, *Federal Reserve Bank of St. Louis Review* 50, 11 (November 1968) 11-23; Comment, by Frank de Leeuw and John Kalchbrinner, and Reply by the authors, ibid., Vol. 51, 4 (May 1969) 6-17; Allan H. Meltzer, Controlling Money, ibid, Vol. 51, 4 (May 1969) 16-24; Emanuel Melicher, Comments on the 'St. Louis position'; Michael W. Keran, Reply, and Leonall C. Andersen, Additional empirical evidence on the reverse-causation argument, ibid., Vol. 51, 7 (August 1969) 16; Michael W. Keran, Monetary and fiscal influences on economic activity – the historical evidence, ibid., Vol. 51, 11 (November 1969) 5-24; David L. Fand, Some issues in monetary economics, ibid., Vol. 52, 1 (January 1970) 10-27; and subsequent contributions.

20 See in particular *Proceedings of a Symposium on Inflation: Its Causes, Consequences and Control*, Stephen W. Rousseas, ed., (Wilton, Connecticut: The Calvin K. Kazanjian Economics Foundation, Inc., 1969).

[21]   See Albert Rees, The Phillips Curve as a menu for policy choice, *Economica,* (NS), 27, 147 (August 1970) 227-38.

[22]   James Tobin, Money and income: Post hoc ergo propter hoc? , *Quarterly Journal of Economics*, 2 (May 1970) 301-17, M. Friedman, Comment on Tobin, ibid., 318-27, and J. Tobin, Reply, ibid., 328-29.

[23]   Milton Friedman, A theoretical framework for a monetary analysis, *Journal of Political Economy* 78, 2 (March-April, 1970) 193-239, and A monetary theory of nominal income, ibid., Vol. 79, 2 (March-April 1971) 323-37; *A Theoretical Framework for Monetary Analysis,* National Bureau of Economic Research Occasional Paper No. 112 (New York: NBER and Columbia University Press, 1971).

[24]   Franco Modigliani, Liquidity preference and the theory of interest and money, *Econometrica* 12, 1 (January 1944) 45-88, reprinted in AEA *Readings in Monetary Theory* (Homewood, Illinois: Richard D. Irwin, 1951). Ch. 11, 186-239.

CHAPTER III

THE MONETARIST APPROACH
TO STABILIZATION POLICY
IN AN OPEN ECONOMY

In the preceding two lectures, I have attempted to discuss some general issues concerning the socio-political causes and consequences of inflation, with the purpose of explaining why inflation of the kind that has been characteristic of the postwar II period and particularly of the past five years or so is not socially conceived of as a problem serious enough for governments to concern themselves with effectively stopping, and to survey briefly the trend of economic theory back towards what is called in contemporary terminology a 'monetarist' explanation of inflation and corresponding prescription of anti-inflationary policy. Unfortunately for the cause of adequate public understanding of the inflation problem of recent years, however, the revival of the quantity theory approach has not gone as far as it should have, and a substantial part of the relevant theory available from the scholarly efforts of our intellectual and professional predecessors remains to be re-discovered and put to effective use. To be concrete, when it came to analysis of the monetary affairs of particular countries, classical and neo-classical monetary theory, represented particularly by David Hume's price-specie-flow mechanism, more or less automatically recognized the linkage of an individual country into a world monetary system through the fixity of exchange rates, and constructed its analysis in terms either of the relation of one country to the whole system or of the behaviour of the system as a whole. Thus, for example, the monetary impact of Spain's conquest of America and despoliation of its precious metals was regarded by scholars of economic history as a European (i.e. world) phenomenon and not merely as a distinguishing eccentric incident in Spanish economic history. But the development of monetary theory since the 1930's, and more specifically since the Keynesian revolution, has tended to focus professional and policy attention on the unique circumstances of individual countries, to the neglect of the international monetary system as an integrated unit. The costs and errors of this excessive atomism of focus of professional attention have become increasingly evident in the international monetary crises of the past decade, culminating in the most recent crisis precipitated by the announcement of President Nixon's "new economic policy" on August 15, 1971, and in the difficulties and futilities that a number of countries have encountered in trying to pursue anti-inflationary policies on an individual national policy basis. It has only gradually begun to dawn on central bankers, in the face of much domestic political incredulousness or active opposition, that inflation is a world and not merely a national problem, and that the first step necessary for an effective anti-inflationary policy is revision or severance of the monetary links between the national and the international monetary systems — and this realization has been impeded by the fact that only a handful of economists specialized on study of the international monetary system as a system have proved competent to give intellectual expression to the problems confronted by central bankers in their practical dealings with one another and with their individual country's problems.[1]

For this situation there have been a number of reasons, inherent on the one hand in the techniques of academic theory construction and development, and on the other hand in the economic history of the world economy since the 1930's. To take the academic side of the picture first, Keynes for understandable theoretical reasons wrote the *General Theory* on the assumption of a closed economy. Consequently, it was left to the international trade theorists to develop models of the international implications of the theory of effective demand; and while they did so fairly quickly and effectively, their models had the central defect of stopping with the determination of the short-run balance-of-payments surplus or deficit, rather than pursuing the monetary and aggregate demand implications of such an international disequilibrium situation; and in any case their work had little influence on the generality of economists, whose thinking remained confined by the closed-economy assumptions of the original Keynesian model. In retrospect, I believe, Keynes can be legitimately and strongly criticized for a sophisticated type of intellectual opportunism — characteristic of the man's personality and philosophy of life — which has had seriously adverse long-run effects both for the welfare of his own country and for the relevance of economics. For, having recognized clearly and protested strongly against the unemployment-creating effects of the decision of his government to return to an over-valued parity for the pound in 1925, he first proposed protection as an employment-creating policy, without adequately placarding its second-best conditionality on the political refusal to contemplate a currency devaluation, and then produced a theory of unemployment which laid the blame for it on the inherent nature of capitalism itself, or by implication on the failure of the authorities to use domestic fiscal and monetary policy effectively, rather than on the international monetary system and on Britain's relations with it. The consequence for British policy-making has been a pronounced and persistent tendency both to regard the country's international economic relations as peripheral and concentrate instead on domestic fiscal and monetary measures as panaceas for the country's chronic problems of international competitive weakness and slow economic growth, and to respond to manifestations of international economic difficulties by various kinds of restrictions on imports of goods and exports of capital, and subsidies — including knighthoods for the individuals concerned — to exports and to domestic production of import substitutes. The failure of this policy approach to solve the country's real problems is fundamentally responsible for the current desperate effort to gain membership in the European Economic Communities, an effort which has been aptly described to me recently as an effort to purchase economic euphoria whatever the long-run cost — the idea of 'Europe' has become the opiate of the English upper classes, distracting them from the problems they have failed to solve into daydreams of a glorious imperial future.

For academic economic theory, Keynes's endorsement of the starting point of a closed economy whose authorities have potentially complete control over its economic destiny has been a powerful distraction from recognition of the reality of an increasingly economically integrated world economy containing an increasing number of economically relevant nations, most of which are atomistic competitors in the world economic system with little if any control over how that system develops. Acceptance of the closed-economy theoretical assumption, despite its obvious irrelevance for most nations, has been powerfully reinforced by the transfer of scientific leadership in economics from the British to the Americans, a people whose near-self-sufficiency economically and economic dominance of world production and investment make the closed-economy assumption less obviously unrealistic and unhelpful to understanding than it is for most other nations. It is one of the paradoxes of the contemporary world — though an understandable one — that so many of its younger economists have been trained in the United States in techniques of analysis which exclude by initial assumption the essential fact of life for their own nation — the dominance of the outside world over their economic destiny — and that it has been left to members of the economics profession from the numerically or economically smaller nations — the Argentinians, the Australians, the Belgians, the Canadians, the Dutch, the Indians, the Pakistanis and the Swedes — to work out the theory of economic policy in an international economic context.[2]

The closed-economy assumption, however, could only have survived as a central theoretical assumption if it fitted the context of theoretical analysis and policy-making as generally understood — and this it did until very recently. The disruption of the international monetary and trading investment system by the Great Depression of 1929 and the 1930's, followed by the second world war and the centralization of economic management that it entailed, resulted in a situation characterized both by nationalism in economic policy thinking and by an uncustomary degree of national economic independence in actual policy making. Under the circumstances, it was natural enough for economic theory to concentrate on analysis based on the closed-economy assumption and to regard international economic relations as an occasional but generally peripheral policy constraint. That situation has gradually changed, as a result of longer-run international economic policies in the fields of monetary organization and trade relationships designed to restore the world economy to an improved version of the liberal economic order of the nineteenth century, adopted as the plan of postwar international economic reconstruction, together with the inevitable progression of international economic integration made possible and indeed dictated by the development of modern technologies of transport and communication. But economic theory as generally understood and practised has been slow to modernise itself.

The standard theory of international economic relations and of economic policy for the government of an open economy seeking to achieve the paired objectives of domestic stability at full employment and a viable balance of payments — international and external balance, in James Meade's classic terminology[3] — is a mixture of the results of the two revolutions of the 1930's — the Keynesian revolution, which contributed the basic principle of determination of the level of employment by aggregate demand operating through the multiplier, and the imperfect competition revolution, which contributed the principle of handling the international trade aspects of aggregate demand by treating trading nations as equivalent to imperfectly competitive firms whose sales volumes depended on the relative prices they charged, these being determined by their assumedly rigid domestic money wage levels and their exchange rates. The latter approach was made unnecessarily mysterious and difficult by treating exports and imports separately and initially in partial equilibrium terms, rather than handling substitutability between domestic and foreign goods in the combined foreign and domestic markets in general equilibrium terms, with a resulting production of elaborate and often incomprehensible formulas for the stability conditions of the system, expressed in strings of elasticities which lent themselves to scepticism about the effectiveness of devaluation, that came to be described as 'elasticity pessimism'. The resulting model, which still dominates official thinking, is a real model and not a monetary model, one in which exchange rate changes or domestic price level changes produce real relative price effects and the monetary effects of both money price level changes and balance-of-payments disequilibria are either ignored or assumed for analytical purposes to be automatically sterilized by monetary policy. Unfortunately, this crucial assumption is almost invariably overlooked by those who apply the model to practical policy problems. Worse still, the practitioners frequently overlook what the theorists have been careful to build into the model, the multiplier reaction of an exchange-rate-change-induced change in the current account on the aggregate demand for domestic goods and services, and the corresponding need for an exchange rate change to be backed up by fiscal and monetary policy changes designed to counteract these effects, instead treating exchange rate changes in partial equilibrium terms as affecting only the foreign trade sector. Both errors of oversight were committed by the British government in connection with the devaluation of the pound in 1967; the result was the to-the-authorities-surprising failure of devaluation to improve the balance of payments as rapidly as predicted, the eventual adoption of severely deflationary measures that account both for the eventual surprising success of devaluation in improving the British balance of payments and for the outburst of wage inflation in the past two years, and — most relevant to this lecture — a conversion of the approach of British policy-making, in part under pressure from the International Monetary Fund, away from orthodox Keynesianism towards an at least nominally monetarist approach·to the use of monetary policy.

That conversion, as far as it has gone, has taken place against the academic background of rapid development of a new, monetarist, approach to the theory of the international monetary system and its mechanics and problems. While the emergence of this new approach has been very largely the work of my colleague

R.A. Mundell and our students at the University of Chicago[4], and harks consciously back to David Hume's analysis of the price-specie-flow mechanism, I believe myself, on the basis admittedly of a hunch derived from the literature rather than of scholarly research, that its intellectual lineage can be traced back, via Mundell's period of service in the research department of the International Monetary Fund under J.J. Polak, to the 1930's work on monetary equilibrium of the Dutch economist J.G. Koopmans and the subsequent development by M.W. Holtrop and the Netherlands Bank of its practical expression in the Bank's model of monetary analysis.[5]

The new monetarist approach differs radically from the standard Keynesian approach to international monetary economics in placing its emphasis fully on the application of monetary theory and taking it off relative national price levels and interest rates as determinants of international flows of goods and capital.[6] In place of the prevailing assumption of imperfect competition between national goods and between national securities, it assumes, for the sake of theoretical simplicity but at the cost of some obnubilation of the fundamental departure of the new theory from the old, which concerns the role of money in the system and not a difference of empirical assumptions about the degree of perfection of international competition, that competition in integrated world commodity and capital markets establishes one world price level to which national price levels must conform, and one world level of interest rates to which national interest rates must conform. This assumption clears the way for a monetary analysis of both world price and interest rate developments and of national stabilization policy alternatives. At the same time, the new approach departs radically from previous analysis of the conditions for monetary equilibrium or monetary neutrality by basing its analysis on the assumption of on-going economic growth rather than of a given endowment of factors of production and a consequently static economy.

The results of the new approach, once one grasps the structure of the basic model, are fairly simply predictable from contemporary monetary theory, but quite radical in their implications.

First, looking at the international monetary system as a whole, the theory says that the rate of inflation in the world economy will be determined by the rate of world monetary expansion relative to the world rate of real economic growth. Using Fisher's theory of the relation between real and money rates of interest, the relative rates of money and real world growth will, once the resulting price trend gets incorporated into expectations, determine the level of money interest rates, these being higher the higher the rate of world monetary expansion (assuming relative constancy of the world real rate of interest). Given the structure of the international monetary system, at least as it existed up to August 15, 1971, as a fixed rate system based on the dollar as international reserve currency, together with the dominance of the United States in world trade, production, and investment, the rate of world monetary expansion and inflation will be governed by the monetary policy of the Federal Reserve System. Further, the theory of the inflation tax suggests, rather ominously, that optimal policy for the United States from the viewpoint of its own economic self-interest is to expand the supply of dollars fast enough to impose some degree of inflation on the rest of the world economy.[7] On the other hand, exploitation of this possibility, or merely the pursuit of an inflationary policy in the United States, obliges the rest of the world to earn a balance-of-payments surplus with the United States somehow — a fact whose inconsistency with other policy objectives of the United States provoked the contemporary international monetary crisis.

The monetary approach to analysis of the international monetary system also suggests that the problem that has preoccupied international monetary experts and commentators for nearly two decades, the alleged prospect of an imminent shortage of international liquidity and need to assure a sufficiently large and rapidly growing world stock of international reserves through new institutional arrangements, is an exact inversion of the real problem of the system, which is to establish international control over the magnitude and rate of growth of international reserves and use it to restrain the rate of growth of those reserves to a non-inflationary pace — assuming that there is a genuine international political will to halt inflation and restore price stability, a subject on which I have earlier expressed some doubts. Further, the monetary approach suggests that the creation of new international reserves — specifically, Special Drawing Rights at the International Monetary Fund — will in the longer run simply accelerate the pace of world inflation, rather than, as its proponents expect, lead countries to hold larger reserves relative to their international trade and payments and on this basis pursue more liberal international economic policies. This proposition, implausible though it may appear to those who have recommended, or been concerned in the negotiations for, the initiation of new international reserve assets, rests firmly on elementary monetary theory as well as on recent work on the optimum quantity of money. The point is that holders of money will hold real balances up to the point where their marginal service yield just compensates for the loss of interest involved in holding money rather than real assets. The alleged shortage of international reserves, which in monetary theory is contradicted by the fact of world inflation, reflects the fact that the very low yield customarily obtaining on international reserve assets and the low rate customarily charged on central bank and I.M.F. loans to countries in balance-of-payments difficulties, together with the tax on reserve-holding implied by inflation itself, make it optimal for countries to keep their reserves relatively low and rely on other, directly interventionist, policies in emergencies. To induce them to hold larger reserves and so free themselves from the need to resort to illiberal balance-of-payments measures it is necessary to make the holding of international reserves more financially attractive. Yet this the S.D.R.s are deliberately designed not to be; and efforts to avoid holding them, or laxity of domestic policies supported by the knowledge that they are not attractive to hold, will necessarily result in inflation and the reduction of their real value.

Turning from the system as a whole to the position of individual countries in it, there is one immediate and obvious implication. So long as countries maintain fixed exchange rates, they cannot in the long run avoid the common rate of inflation. The only way to do so is by repeated currency appreciation, or flotation of the exchange rate. There is a further, less obvious corollary: if a country maintains its fixed exchange rate but tries to stop inflation by the usual methods of fiscal and monetary restraint, it is highly likely to wind up with the worst possible of results, unabated inflation combined with unemployment of men and productive capacity. This corollary, however, it should be noted, involves a modification of the model for the short-run application of it, since the assumption of perfect international mobility of goods and capital implies that neither fiscal nor monetary policy can exercise any influence over aggregate economic activity: all that fiscal policy can do in abstract principle is to determine the size and composition of government expenditure and the proportion of it financed by debt, and all that monetary policy can do is to determine the aggregate amount of bank credit (subject to limits to be discussed below) and, depending on policy, who gets the benefit of it.

This brings me to the fundamental point, that in this model, at least as a long-run proposition, the central bank has no control over the supply of money. This is an extremely important point, given the fact that so much monetary theory and empirical analysis has been conducted in terms of the supply of money as the key economic variable and policy instrument; and it is one that monetary economists outside the United States, and particularly those working on small open economies, should be especially wary of, since the self-sufficiency of the U.S. economy makes its money supply more nearly a policy-controlled variable than can be safely assumed for other countries — and most of our models of monetary analysis come from research on the United States economy and monetary system.

The reason is that, on the assumptions of the model, the public can adjust the nominal supply of money to what it wants by exporting or importing money through the balance of payments. This is in contrast to the theory of money in a closed economy, in which the monetary authority controls the nominal quantity of money and the public adjusts its real balances to what it wants through spending behaviour affecting the price level. In the posited circumstances, the central bank's actions control only the division of the assets backing the money supply set by the public between domestic credit and international reserves. (The limitation of the total of these assets to the money supply desired by the public sets the limits mentioned earlier to the capacity of the central bank to vary the total of domestic bank credit.) In the context of a growing economy, central banking policy determines how far the growth of the public's demand for money is provided for by domestic credit expansion, and how far it must be provided for by a balance-of-payments surplus. (Alternatively, of course, excessive domestic credit expansion leads to a balance-of-payments deficit.) For a very simple aggregative model[8], the relationship can be expressed in the following formula:

$$g_R = \frac{1}{r}\left(\eta_{my}g_y + g_p\right) - \frac{1-r}{r}g_C,$$

where g_R is the growth rate of the country's reserves, r is the ratio of international reserves to domestic money supply, η_{my} is the income-elasticity of demand for real balances, g_y the growth-rate of output, g_p the rate of world inflation, and g_C the growth-rate of domestic credit. The formula implies, contrary to some Keynesian theory but in conformity with observation, that other things being equal the faster a country grows the more favourable its balance of payments will be, and contrary to some other Keynesian theory that looks to demand pressure to stimulate

90

productivity growth and improve the balance of payments, that more rapid domestic credit expansion worsens the balance of payments, a result also in conformity with observation. The model can easily be disaggregated to produce predictions about the behaviour of the separate accounts of the balance of payments: on the assumption that faster growth requires the investment of more real resources, more rapid growth will involve a deterioration of the current account and a more than offsetting improvement of the capital account, a result which also accords with the facts of experience.

A further point about the model is that, from the standpoint of its effects on the balance of payments (and, in a less rigidly full employment version of the model, on the domestic economy) currency devaluation or depreciation has precisely the same effects (apart from a weighting coefficient) as a deflation of domestic credit — as can be seen by assuming stable world prices and interpreting g_p in the above formula as the (instantaneous) rate of change of the domestic price of foreign exchange. Moreover, the effect of devaluation is transitory, working through the restoration of the public's actual to its desired real balances via the impact of an excess demand for money in producing a surplus on the current or capital accounts, or both, of the balance of payments; its effects can be offset by a simultaneous increase in the rate of domestic credit expansion; and it entails an inflation of domestic money prices to the extent of the devaluation. A continuing balance-of-payments surplus requires either repeated devaluation, or continuing restraint on the rate of growth of domestic credit.

These observations provide a theoretical basis for both the well-known preference of central bankers for monetary restraint over currency depreciation as a means of correcting a balance-of-payments deficit, and the belief frequently encountered among businessmen that devaluation will be of little lasting help in improving their international competitive position because it will be quickly followed by a corresponding wage inflation. Both these views appear, in the light of the Keynesian model of devaluation, to be firmly rooted in invincible economic ignorance. And indeed, the proposition that devaluation is deflationary and its corollary that appreciation is inflationary appear wildly paradoxical from a Keynesian-theoretical point of view. But the Keynesian point of view can be faulted, as already noted, for identifying exchange rate changes with changes in real relative prices and for ignoring the monetary implications of currency depreciations and appreciations. Further, with respect to the monetary model of exchange rate policy it should be noted that the adjectives 'deflationary' and 'inflationary' refer to the monetary effects of exchange rate change and not to the price level effects, which run in the customary direction familiar to common sense. However, in the monetary model, contrary to the Keynesian model, these price level effects are a direct consequence of the assumption that countries are close competitors in international trade and finance and do not require the activation of the intermediary mechanism of an increase or decrease in domestic production and employment.

As a final comment on the subject of exchange rate adjustment, it may be remarked that the monetarist and Keynesian theories of the balance of payments have conflicting implications for the long-standing question, invented in the 1930's with respect to the gold standard, revived in recent years with respect to the fixed-rate 'adjustable peg' I.M.F. system, and raised in an acute form recently by President Nixon's 'new economic policy', of whether the established international monetary system contains a deflationary or an inflationary bias, as reflected in the question whether the system puts relatively and significantly more pressure on deficit countries to devalue or on surplus countries to appreciate. Contrary to the accepted Keynesian (and Nixonian) view of the matter, the monetarist view suggests that a revealed preference of members of the international monetary community of nations for devaluations rather than revaluations is inflationary rather than deflationary for the system as a whole, for the admittedly rather complicated and not entirely logically water-tight reason that the availability of devaluation as a policy alternative encourages nations to economize on their international reserves, and that the predictable inflationary consequences of probable devaluations encourage the public to economize on its money holdings.

The reason is not entirely logically water-tight because the basic theory makes the world rate of inflation in terms of world market prices a function of the relation between the growth rate of world monetary reserves and the growth rate of real world output, and the influences mentioned affect neither of these directly. However, one might argue in Keynesian terms that the deflationary policies that usually precede and provide a ceremonially adequate reason for devaluation have the average effect of reducing the rate of real economic growth, while the reluctance of governments to commit themselves or insist on others committing themselves to the politically shameful act of devaluation inclines them both to favour measures accelerating the growth rate of international monetary reserves and to collaborate in the innovation of successive new methods of substituting national and international credit arrangements for basic international money that reduce the rate of growth of the stock of such money required to accommodate real world economic growth at stable world prices. In any case, as already mentioned, the alleged 'deflationary bias' of the present (i.e. up to August 15, 1971) international monetary system is at complete variance with the empirically observed facts of over a quarter century of chronic world price inflation.

The ideas involved in the new monetarist approach to balance-of-payments and international monetary theory can, as I have already suggested, probably be traced back at least in part to the Dutch monetary theorizing of the 1930's and 1940's; in any case they are very similar in fundamental respects to the model of monetary analysis developed by M.W. Holtrop and employed by the Netherlands Bank. When I first came across a summary of the theoretical foundations of that model, however — in a French-language work largely on Keynesian theory by Emile Claassen[9] — I was puzzled by what appeared to me to be an illegitimate mixture of stock and flow analysis. My early reading in preparation for these lectures did not dispel my puzzlement — which incidentally stems from my Keynesian background and not from the concern of my friend Professor Frits de Jong with the question of dimensionality in economics[10] and with dimensional inconsistency in the earlier versions of the Holtrop–Bank model.[11] However, by virtue of having read some recent and important papers by Holtrop and de Jong[12], I have convinced myself that the model cannot be accused of logical error, though it can still be accused of being unnecessarily subtle and complex, as well as potentially misleading to unwary students, from the standpoint of recent developments of monetary theory. These criticisms pertain to the international aspects of the model, and not to the domestic aspects, which incorporate a fairly simple practical application of Keynes's distinction between transactions and liquidity balances and which I shall ignore; and the counter-argument and defense against them is, quite acceptably as a compromise between practical and theoretical gentlemen like ourselves, that the

model is intended to be a means of interpreting monetary developments in the past year of experience as a
guide to policy-making for the next year, and not a
rigorous and academically impeccable statement of
the underlying monetary theory. Nevertheless, I shall
devote the rest of the lecture to comments on that
model.

I begin with some comments intended as much for
my own use as for the enlightenment of my audience,
on the standard Keynesian multiplier theory for an
open economy in a fixed exchange rate system, as
developed in the 1930's and 1940's very quickly after
the publication of Keynes's *General Theory*. According to that theory, an exogenous increase in
foreign demand for exports (ΔX) had a multiplier
effect in increasing domestic income (ΔY) according
to the formula $\Delta Y = \frac{\Delta X}{(m+s)}$, where m is the marginal
propensity to import and s is the marginal propensity
to save. In Keynesian theory, s is a flow relationship
between saving and income; but postwar theorists
realized, not always clearly, that in the context of an
open economy it has to be defined not only as the net
difference of the two relationships between saving and
income and investment and income — an obvious
point, but one that frequently overlooked the fact
that the concept of a 'propensity to invest' fails to
capture the essence of the acceleration principle, since
the latter relates investment to the rate of change of
income and not to its level — but also as a net income-
related propensity to accumulate, and not merely to

hold, cash. The difference is a vital one in monetary theory, because monetary theory, including the Keynesian theory of a closed economy, has always held that the level of money income determines, or at least helps to determine, the stock of cash people want to hold, but *not* the rate of increase of the stock of cash people want to hold, which in terms of the same theory is determined by the rate of increase and not the current level of money income.

The Keynesian multiplier models for an international economy therefore — as contrasted at least with the more sophisticated closed-economy multiplier models — rested on a confusion of stock-adjustment and flow behaviour. This could however be justified on two grounds. The first, made particularly explicit in the concluding chapter of the seminal classic monograph by Fritz Machlup[13], and reflected in recent years in theoretical and empirical work employing the concept of 'the basic balance of payments' or of 'international financial intermediation', is that economic analysis of international economic phenomena should concern itself with the 'real' realities of production, consumption, and international transfers of real resources, and that the question of whether or not real international resource flows are financed by flows of loans at interest, and hence constitute no problem for economic policy, or by flows of international reserves, and hence constitute a balance-of-payments problem, is a matter of financial detail and financial policy not deserving the attention of a serious economist. On this argument, the assumption of a constant net saving rate applying to the acquisition of international assets was a legitimate demarcation of the line between economic reality and the financial froth that distracted the policy-makers from proper economic analysis and understanding. The alternative defense, which can be put with less or more theoretical sophistication concerning the dynamics of stock-flow adjustments, is that the assumption of a fixed relationship between the hoarding of international money and the level of domestic money income is an approximation to a more complicated theory of money demand that is legitimate and useful for the length of the time-period to which the analysis is intended to apply.

Whatever one thinks of the acceptability of these rationalizations of the Keynesian procedure for formulating multiplier theory for an open economy, one must I think be initially surprised by and suspicious of the appearance of what looks like a very similar formula in the Dutch theoretical model, which formula I shall write as

$$\Delta Y = \frac{E}{m + k},$$

where E is described as the 'external monetary impulse' and k as a version of the familiar 'Cambridge k' of monetary theory. There are two reasons for surprise and suspicion. First, in contrast to the Keynesian multiplier formula, E seems to represent the level of a flow magnitude and not a change in the level of that flow; and second, k is not a Keynesian propensity relating the flow demand for the accumulation of cash balances to the flow level of income, but a classical behaviour relationship relating the level of stock demand for money to the flow level of income, which should exercise only a transitory influence on the determination of income and expenditure flows and make no appearance in a multiplier formula relating domestic money income to external monetary impulses. To be theoretically crude and literarily blunt about the point, a Keynesian model of income determination, based on the assumption of perfectly elastic supply of domestic resources at constant money prices, crossed with a quantity theory (or even a properly interpreted Keynesian theory) of the demand for money in which demand for and supply of money eventually reach equality, should lead to one of Machlup's simplest formulas,

$$\Delta Y = \frac{\Delta X}{m},$$

which asserts simply that the balance of payments has to balance when the public has acquired the money supply that its current income level leads it to demand. Alternatively, if classical wage and price flexibility assumptions are employed to ensure full employment in real terms, together with the same long-run assumption of satisfaction of demand for real cash balances, and stability of foreign prices is not assumed, we obtain the result, now defining ΔY as the change in money income in response to once-over comparative-static changes in domestic productivity and the world money price level and abstracting from imperfect competition possibilities,

$$\Delta Y \approx p\Delta X + X\Delta p,$$

where ΔX is the increase in domestic real productive capacity and Δp is the increase in the world price level.

The doubts and suspicions, however, are resolved when one recognizes three points that are not altogether clear — or perhaps more fairly are hidden in plain sight in the literary and statistical descriptions of the Dutch model — namely that the model is not a Keynesian-style multiplier—equilibrium model of the familiar Anglo-Saxon kind but an interpretative model pertaining to one period only of a dynamic process extending over a sequence of periods; that the adjustment of current money demand to current income is assumed to occur during the period under analysis; and, most important, that the concept of 'external monetary impulse' is exactly what it says — the total autonomous flow of money into the economy from abroad in the period, and not, as in the Keynesian model, the change in aggregate foreign purchases from the economy since the previous period. (It is also important to recognize — a point that Keynesian and probably most quantity theorists would quibble with

— that all such money inflows are assumed to go either into spending or into an accumulation of cash balances related only to increases in income — though the implications of the assumption that inflows of cash balances from abroad will be held and not spent only if a rise in income increases the demand for money are probably neutralized by the treatment of changes in the 'hoarding' as distinct from the 'transactions' demand for money as exogenous and unexplained in the model.)

In this formal theoretical framework, which is quite different from both the comparative-static framework of conventional international trade multiplier theory and the equilibrium-growth-path framework of the monetary model of international economic policy presented above, not to speak of the framework of a possible fully-dynamic monetarist model of short-run monetary disturbances in an open economy, the Holtrop–Bank model does turn out to be perfectly logical, as may I hope be seen from the following algebra:

$$
\begin{aligned}
M_{st}^{f} &= X_t + K_t - M_t \\
&= \Delta X_t + X_{t-1} + K_t - M_{t-1} - \Delta M_t \\
&= \Delta X_t + (X_{t-1} - M_{t-1}) + K_t - \Delta M_t \\
&= \Delta X_t + (X_{t-1} - M_{t-1}) + K_t - m\Delta Y_t \\
&= E_t - m\Delta Y_t.
\end{aligned}
$$

Here M_{st}^{f} is the net flow addition to the money supply during the current period, consisting of the difference between the sum of the values of exports and capital inflows during the period and the value of imports during the period; the values of exports and imports during the current period are decomposed into their values in the previous period and the changes in the present period as compared with the previous period; the sum of the increase in exports, the net capital inflow, and the difference between exports and imports in the previous period — described as "any existing current account surplus, carried over from the previous period"[14] — is described as "the total of external monetary impulses" (the autonomous external injection of money into the economy) symbolized by E_t; and the residual negative item, the increase in the current-period value of imports, is assumed to be induced by the change in current income over the previous period operating through a stable marginal import propensity. The net acquisition of money by the economy from abroad (B, the 'national liquidity surplus' or increase in foreign assets held by the banking system) is determined by the requirement that it be equal to the increase in the demand for cash balances induced by the increase in income during the period, i.e.

$$M_{dt}^{f} = k \Delta Y_t \,,$$

where k is the Cambridge constant relating money stock held to income flow and M_{dt}^{f} is the flow demand for money in the period. By simple algebra

102

we arrive finally at the result,

$$Y_t = \frac{E_t}{m + k},$$

from which we started our enquiry. But I hope we now understand how we got there, and that while what we seem to have is something that looks like a Keynesian multiplier formula it is actually nothing of the kind. In fact, if we ignore capital inflows and assume an initial starting point at a balanced current account, together with the Keynesian assumption of an elastic supply of output at current prices, what we have in the Holtrop–Bank model is the dynamic system

$$mY_t + k(Y_t - Y_{t-1}) = X_t.$$

This is simply a first-order difference equation of a long-familiar kind. For the case of a constant level of exports (X), the solution is of the form

$$Y_t = A\,a^t + Z,$$

where a, obtained from the homogeneous part (or characteristic equation) of the difference equation, is equal to $\frac{k}{(m+k)}$; Z, obtained by substitution for Y_t and Y_{t-1} in the original equation, is equal to $\overline{X}/m$; and the constant A is obtained from the solution for $t=0$, and is equal to $(Y_0 - \frac{X}{m})$. Hence the solution is

$$Y_t = \frac{\overline{X}}{m} - (\frac{\overline{X}}{m} - Y_0)\,(\frac{k}{k+m})^t.$$

103

The second term on the right hand side vanishes with time, so that income converges on the level at which imports become equal to exports in the long run. For purposes of comparative statics analysis, it is convenient to assume that the economy has become adjusted to a certain level of exports, so that $Y_0 = \frac{X_0}{m}$, and that the level of exports rises by $\bar{x}$. Defining $y_t = Y_t - Y_0$, the equation becomes

$$y_t = \frac{\bar{x}}{m} - \frac{\bar{x}}{m} \left(\frac{k}{k+m}\right)^t,$$

the second term on the right vanishing over time as in the original equation. This equation implies that the economy can only have a continuing growth of income, as well as a continuing balance-of-payments surplus ($m\, y_t < \bar{x}$) if exports are continuously rising, and that the surplus will be relatively greater the faster the increase of exports (and therefore of income).

To explore the subject further, assume that exports grow by the fraction g per period (i.e. $X_t = X_0 (1+g)^t$) and utilize the convergence properties of the equation to justify concentration on the long-run equilibrium in which income and exports grow at the same rate. Then

$$Y_{t-1} = \frac{1}{1+g}\, Y_t,$$

and from the equation

$$Y_t = \frac{1+g}{m + mg + kg}\, X_t,$$

$$B_t = X_t - mY_t = \frac{kg}{m + mg + kg} X_t,$$

$$\frac{B_t}{Y_t} = \frac{kg}{1 + g},$$

$$\frac{B_t}{X_t} = \frac{kg}{m + mg + kg}.$$

It is easily shown that $\frac{B_t}{Y_t}$ and $\frac{B_t}{X_t}$, the two obvious measures of the relative size of the balance-of-payments surplus, both increase with both k, the money-to-income ratio, and g, the rate of growth of export demand which in the model determines the rate of growth of domestic income. Thus the model produces the same results as the monetary model presented above, positive association between the growth rate of output and the balance-of-payments surplus, though in the former model growth was assumed to be autonomously determined while in this model it is export-led.

I should perhaps apologize to my audience for taking them through an exercise in theoretical exegesis and interpretation dictated by personal curiosity about the intellectual bridges and consistencies among three theoretical approaches — the Dutch, the Keynesian, and the monetarist — to a common problem in international monetary dynamics, especially as I can glory in the discovery of no theoretical errors embarrassing to those who invited me here to discuss a subject in which I know they have had a more long-sustained intellectual interest than I have.

But I happen to believe that intellectual bridges are important. The world of scholarship is too small and too fragile for scholars in different countries to ignore — or worse, deliberately reject — the opportunity to learn from one another's understanding of the legacy of the long tradition of economic scholarship and attempts to apply it to the elucidation of the laws and meaning of economic reality. I have been deeply grateful for, and have benefitted from, the challenge to survey the contemporary state of monetary theory and the theory of inflation, before an audience of scholars who have held more firmly to the long tradition of European monetary theory than have those trained like myself in the contemporary literature and traditions of English-language economics. I hope only that the results of our joint labours through this series of lectures will contribute something to our common understanding of the real issues that confront us.

NOTES

[1] The undisputed dean of economists specializing on the problems of the international monetary system is, of course, Robert Triffin of Yale, though this fact has often been obscured in academic controversy by the natural propensity of the scientific community to undervalue the importance of recognition of a problem and overvalue the display of elegance, worldly wisdom and professional dispassionateness in arriving at its solution.

[2] A small sample of the relevant names would include Sidrauski;

Corden, Kemp, McDougall, and Swan; Drèze; Asimakopoulos, Eastman, English, Safarian, Slater, Smith and Stykolt, to mention only resident Canadians; Stuvel and Tinbergen; Bardhan, Bhagwati, Desai, Ramaswami, and Srinivasan; Islam, Haq, and Naqvi; and Linder. Mention must be made also, however, of the great contributions of James Meade, both as a writer of theory and as a teacher of such students as Corden, Lancaster, Lipsey, Mundell, Ozga, and Rybczynski, while he was Professor at the London School of Economics; and of the influence of the ubiquitous genius of P.A. Samuelson, the incorrigible curiosity of C.P. Kindleberger, and the scholarly devotion of such transplanted European scholars as William Fellner, Gottfried Haberler, Fritz Machlup, Tibor Scitovszky, and Robert Triffin in keeping international economic theory alive in the United States.

3   J.E. Meade, *The Theory of International Economic Policy. Vol.I: The Balance of Payments* (London: Macmillan, 1951).

4   See especially R.A. Mundell, *International Economics* (New York: Macmillan, 1968), Chs. 8 and 9.

5   Again, I acknowledge my indebtedness to the monograph by Frits J. de Jong and the evaluative essay by Marius W. Holtrop cited at the beginning of my first lecture.

6   For a fuller discussion of the new approach and analysis of its departures from traditional monetary theory, see my The Monetary Approach to Balance-of-Payments Theory; for an application of it to the current inflationary situation, see my Inflation: A Monetarist View; both will be reprinted in my forthcoming *Further Essays in Monetary Economics* (London: Allen and Unwin, 1972).

7   See R.A. Mundell, The optimum balance of payments deficit and the value of empires, prepared for the Conference on Stabilization Policies in Interdependent Economies, University of Paris–Dauphine, March 25–27, 1971 (forthcoming in the proceedings of the Conference).

8   The model involves the behaviour assumption about the demand for money

$$M_d = p\,f(Y)$$

where the interest rate is assumed fixed by world forces and suppressed into the functional form, Y is real output, and the multiplicative factor p, representing the world price level, embodies the homogeneity postulate of the main stream of classical monetary theory; the balance-sheet identity for the money supply,

$$M_S = R + C,$$

where R represents international reserves or foreign assets and C domestic credit or domestic assets held by the (consolidated) banking system; and the equilibrium condition, assumed to be instantaneously satisfied due to the perfection of the world goods and capital markets,

$$M_S = M_d.$$

In terms of growth rates,

$$g_{M_d} = \eta_{my}\, g_y + g_p = g_{M_s} = r\, g_R + (1-r)\, g_C,$$

Where η_{my} is the income elasticity of demand for real balances and

$$r = \frac{R}{(R+C)}$$

The equation in the text is a rearrangement of this one.

[9]   E.M. Claassen, *Monnaie, Revenu National et Prix* (Paris: Dunod, 1968), Ch. I.

[10]   Frits J. de Jong, *Dimensional Analysis for Economists* (Amsterdam: North Holland, 1967).

[11]   See de Jong, Developments of monetary theory in the Netherlands, op. cit., for an account of the criticism and of the subsequent conceptual revision of the statistical model.

[12]   Cited at the beginning of the first lecture.

[13]   Fritz Machlup, *International Trade and the National Income Multiplier* (Philadelphia: Blakiston, 1943).

[14]   Holtrop, op. cit., p.4.